THE

LAST OF THE LENAPÉ,

AND

OTHER POEMS.

BY SAMUEL M. JANNEY.

———

PHILADELPHIA:
HENRY PERKINS—134 CHESTNUT ST.

BOSTON:
PERKINS & MARVIN—114 WASHINGTON ST.

1839.

J. Richards, Printer,
130 N. Third St.

Printing Statement:

Due to the very old age and scarcity of this book,
many of the pages may be hard to read due to the
blurring of the original text, possible missing pages,
missing text, dark backgrounds and other issues
beyond our control.

Because this is such an important and rare work, we
believe it is best to reproduce this book regardless of
its original condition.

Thank you for your understanding.

THE LAST OF THE LENAPÉ,

AND

OTHER POEMS.

CONTENTS.

PREFACE.

In bringing before the public this volume of Poems, the author feels it due to himself to observe that many of them were composed early in life; but the two principal poems, which stand first in the collection, as well as most of the scientific, and some of the descriptive pieces, are of recent production. He trusts that they will all be found calculated to promote the cause of piety and truth, which was the original design of poetry, and ought still to be the main object of its cultivation.

To convey instruction through the medium of pleasing images and delightful associations, is the noblest task of the poet; and although the author of these pages may not possess the power of rising to the highest flights of genius, he is conscious of having endeavoured to improve the abilities entrusted to him,—and it remains with the public to decide upon the merits of his labours.

Occoquan, Va. 12th mo. 4th, 1838.

AN ESSAY ON POETRY.

THERE have been periods when an essay in defence of Poetry, would have been deemed as superfluous as an attempt to defend the cultivation of flower gardens and orchards; but in this utilitarian age, the wonderful discoveries of science, the progress of civil liberty, and the rapid march of improvement in the mechanic arts, in manufactures, and in navigation, have turned the attention of the public almost entirely to those pursuits which minister to the physical wants of man. It is not the design of this essay to discourage those pursuits, but merely to show that there are others which relate more immediately to the wants of the mind, and which have an equal, if not a still greater tendency to extend the sphere of human enjoyment. The happiness of man does not depend so much upon the extent of his temporal possessions, as upon the purity of his desires, and the harmonious action of his moral and intellectual powers. The proper regulation of these powers depends much upon early associations, and upon a refined

2

taste which enables us to enjoy the grand and beautiful in nature, and teaches us to appreciate those ennobling qualities of the mind and of the heart, which constitute the real dignity of man.

There is something so intrinsically beautiful in a life spent in innocence and peace amid the shades of rural retirement, that it has in all ages formed the favourite theme of the moral poet; and there are few men of cultivated minds, however they may be engrossed by the business of life, who do not indulge the hope that they will one day retire from the world, and realize those visions of happiness so long and so fondly cherished. These views, although they may never be realized in actual experience, have still a favourable influence upon the heart, and prevent its tender sensibilities from being entirely destroyed by the withering influence of a worldly spirit. If such minds could trace back the current of their thoughts to the source from whence those associations were derived, they would often find it to be from the perusal, in their youthful days, of some poem, in which the beauties of nature, and the happiness of rural life, were themes of praise.

These effects may likewise be produced by compositions in prose, conveying to the mind the same kind of impressions,—but verse, if well executed, has many advantages over prose, especially as a medium to convey moral sentiments to the young. There is a natural taste in all young persons for the melody of verse,—

they generally show a fondness for the rhymes, the metre, and the alliteration of poetry, before they are capable of appreciating the beauty of the sentiments it conveys.

As the youthful mind advances in knowledge, the taste for metrical composition generally increases in proportion as the capacity to perceive the higher beauties of style, becomes enlarged and improved. Perhaps there is no season in which we enjoy those pleasures with a higher relish, than just before that period arrives when we are to enter upon the arduous duties of life. After the cares of business, and the intercourse of the world, have in some degree worn off the sensibilities of youth, we are apt not only to lose for a season, our relish for literature, but even to find impaired, our love for the beautiful scenery of nature. But that love, if it has once taken root, will again revive, and may in after life, become one of the sources of our highest enjoyment. For whether a man be successful or unsuccessful in the pursuit of worldly objects, he will find at last that the bright anticipations of happiness which he indulged in early life, are not to be realized in the acquisition of wealth or power; and after having joined the crowd in their eager pursuit, he will, if he attends to the admonitions of experience, endeavour to attain the object of his desire in the calm and tranquil enjoyments of domestic life. Then he will find the tastes of his youth again revived; and if in early life he has imbibed a relish for intellectual and spiritual enjoyments, they will become the solace of his declining years.

But there are persons who object to the reading of poetry, because of the wild and extravagant fictions with which it abounds, and the impure images it sometimes conveys.   This objection will apply equally well to compositions in prose, and until the public shall learn to discriminate, and to encourage only that which is good, we must expect the evil to continue.   There is, however, no necessity for resorting to such means for entertainment, for the records of past ages, the traditions of our fathers, and the scenes of real life now acting around us, furnish the poet with abundant materials for the construction of his works.   There is no necessity laid upon him to depart from the truth in his narratives or descriptions;—but like the historical painter, who takes his figures from real life, and places them in attitudes suited for the performance of some action related in authentic history,—although the characters may be copies from nature, yet the attitudes, the grouping, the expression, and the drapery, are his own—and these furnish him all the scope for the exercise of his talent that can be desired.

It does not however follow, because a story is true that it is therefore suitable for poetry, or even for instructive prose,—for some incidents are too trivial, and others too low or disgusting, to be introduced, and it requires a discriminating taste to copy from real life, and

yet to furnish a picture that shall at once afford pleasure
and instruction. Fidelity to nature, and purity of moral
sentiments, ought to be required of every author who
aspires to public favour,—but it must be acknowledged,
that many modern writers in prose and verse, are sadly
deficient in both of these qualifications. It was re-
marked some years ago, by an able writer in one of
the foreign Magazines, "that in perusing some of the
most popular English productions of the present day,
it is impossible not to observe to what an extent our
literature has been infected by the system of substitu-
ting the turbulence and sophistries of lawless passion,
for the delineation of those more regular and decent
movements, which appeal to our sympathy through our
moral approbation. In our poets and our poetical novel
writers, this innovation has been most flagrant and sys-
tematic, and most successful as far as to be read with
avidity, and applauded by the *unthinking*, can constitute
success. The fashionable notion now is, that in a work
of true genius, every thing must be made subordinate to
passion, no matter how unnatural or presumptuous a
tone it may assume; and accordingly, our recent litera-
ture has teemed with impassioned railers against the
decencies of life,—impassioned marauders by sea and
land,—impassioned voluptuaries,—impassioned rene-
gadoes—impassioned striplings—impassioned hags:—
all of them venting furious sublimity upon the astonish-
ed reader, and boldly demanding his profound admira-

2*

tion, because they have lost all control over their actions and words." *

It must be acknowledged that there is a class of writers, of whom this picture is a faithful portrait,—men who have devoted the energies of the loftiest genius, to decorate the couch of voluptuousness, to conceal the deformity of vice, and to strew with the flowers of poesy, the path that leads to destruction. The personages who figure in their pages, although invested with much of heroic sentiment,—would, if they lived and moved among us, be considered the most dangerous associates: and can they be proper subjects for contemplation to the inexperienced mind? There may be characters found or imagined of the most flagrant wickedness,—yet having some traits that bear a resemblance to virtue,—and it is in the power of a vivid imagination, by dwelling upon these, to shed around them a deceptive light which dazzles the beholder.

How many a youthful mind has followed with enthusiasm the story of some imaginary hero, through all the vicissitudes of a career stained with crime. His deeds of cruelty, his relentless hate, and his unbridled passions, are lightly passed over, while the imagination is dazzled by " deeds of noble daring," by a boundless generosity, and by an impassioned devotion to some fair being who leans on him for protection.

* Campbell's Magazine, vol. 1, p. 397.

Such characters have been portrayed by many of the poets and novelists of modern times, and their effects upon the youthful reader cannot fail to be injurious;— if they do not in direct terms encourage vice, they at least sap the foundation of virtue.

But the poets and the novelists are not alone obnoxious to this charge, for even the historian has too often followed in the same path, and bestowed upon personal bravery, that praise which is only due to moral greatness. In casting the mind's eye over the literature of past ages, how much do we find that is calculated to encourage the spirit of war, and how little that tends to cherish the christian virtues. Some of our earliest impressions derived from poetry and history, are inimical to the meek and peaceable spirit of the gospel. "We are intoxicated with the exploits of the conqueror as recorded in real history or in glowing fiction. We follow with a sympathetic ardour, his rapid and triumphant career in battle, and, unused as we are to suffering and death, forget the fallen and miserable who are crushed under his victorious car. Particularly by the study of the ancient poets and historians, the sentiments of early and barbarous ages on the subject of war are kept alive in the mind. The trumpet which roused the fury of Achilles, and of the hordes of Greece, still resounds in our ears, and though *christians by profession*, some of our earliest and deepest impressions are received in

the school of uncivilized antiquity."* May we not hope
that the benign influence of the gospel of Christ, and
the increasing light of civilization, will yet more and
more influence mankind, until we shall have a litera-
ture suited to the wants of a christian people. A litera-
ture that instead of rousing the warlike passions, and
inciting the love of worldly glory, will tend to soothe
the perturbed spirit, and inspire the contemplative mind
with a relish for piety, harmony and peace. It appears
to me that such a day must yet arrive, and he who
would write for posterity, must cultivate in his own
mind, and endeavour to impress upon his works, those
sentiments which are suited for a purer and a happier
age. In these views I am supported by one of the
greatest of modern poets, who says,

> " Noise, is there not enough in doleful war,
> But that the heaven-born poet must stand forth
> And lend the echoes of his sacred shell,
> To multiply and aggravate the din?
> Pangs, are there not enough in hopeless love;
> And in requited passion, all too much
> Of turbulence, anxiety and fear,
> But that the minstrel of the rural shade
> Must tune his pipe insidiously, to nurse
> The perturbation in the suffering breast,
> And propagate its kind where e'er he may?"

* Channing's Discourse on War.

Ah! who (and with such rapture as befits
The hallowed theme) will rise and celebrate
The good man's deeds and purposes, retrace
His struggles, his discomfiture deplore,
His triumphs hail, and glorify his end."

WORDSWORTH.

It is not favourable to virtue, for the mind to dwell
too much upon scenes of depravity and guilt, whether
they be described in authentic history, or portrayed in
glowing colours by the novelist or the poet. But let us
rather contemplate the beautiful and sublime in nature,
and the wise and benevolent in human life,—and more
especially let us keep ever in our view the glorious
benignity of the divine character, as exhibited in the
works of creation, and taught and exemplified by Jesus
Christ.

" For the attentive mind
By this harmonious action on her powers,
Becomes herself harmonious: wont so oft
In outward things to meditate the charm
Of sacred order, soon she seeks at home
To find a kindred order, to exert
Within herself this elegance of love,
This fair inspir'd delight: her temper'd powers
Refine at length, and every passion wears
A chaster, milder, more attractive mien."

AKENSIDE.

We shall then find that poetry of the highest order will
find a response in our own feelings, and be like a mir-

ror to present to our view the images of our past emo-
tions,—for true poetic feeling is not confined to the
bosom of the poet,—it is felt at times by every pure
and elevated mind, when placed in circumstances favour-
able for its development.   For instance, when, retired
from the bustle of the world and surrounded by beauti-
ful and tranquil scenery, we muse upon the uncertainty
of life and think upon the dear companions of our child-
hood who have passed away from this scene of exist-
ance.   Who is there that does not realize on such an
occasion, that impassioned feeling which is the soul of
poetry?   The impressions which are thus made upon
the mind may lie concealed for years, but if we meet
with a passage by which they are revived, or by which
kindred associations are produced, how delightful it is
to hear the harmonious numbers sounding in our ears
like the echoes of the past.   But although these emo-
tions which are poetical in their nature, may at times
prevail in almost every mind, it must be conceded that
the power of describing them so as to convey their im-
ages distinctly to others, is a faculty possessed by few;
and in this faculty chiefly consists the characteristic of
the poet.

If this view be correct, it would seem that although
poetry, *as an art*, must be confined to a few, yet the
cultivation of poetic feelings and associations is open
for all; and there can be no doubt it was intended by
the benificent Author of our being, to be a source of

refined and exalted enjoyment. And this enjoyment
does not depend entirely upon the beauty of language,
or the harmony of verse,—although these have confer-
red upon it additional charms,—it depends chiefly upon
that harmony of the mind,—that music of the soul,—
which is independent of audible sounds, and which
may be felt by the contemplative mind to draw us
away from the things of time, and to direct our thoughts
to that region of sublime enjoyment, where every heart
will be attuned to harmony and love.

> " Thus the men
> Whom nature's works can charm, with God himself
> Hold converse; grow familiar day by day
> With his conceptions; act upon his plan,
> And form to his the relish of their souls."
>
> AKENSIDE

DEDICATION.

To THEE, dear Wife! I dedicate the strain
   By which has oft been cheer'd our loneliest hours,
When, like a frost, untimely grief and pain
   Came o'er the heart, to blight the fairest flowers:
   When, in the spring, to their deserted bowers
The birds return, we hail their cheering lays,
   Then let us not despise those nobler powers,
By which the muse the drooping soul can raise,
And fill the thoughtful mind with gratitude and praise.

'Tis not an idle song, I here present,
   The wildering fires of passion to impart,
But fram'd with higher views,—and with intent
   To wake the finer feelings of the heart:
   For 'tis the province of the minstrel's art,
(A noble art when worthily pursued;)
   To soothe the anguish left by sorrow's dart,
To cheer the lonely hours of solitude,
And fill the soul with love for all that's great and good.

   3

How pure the pleasure that pervades the mind,
.   When Cowper's verse, and Gray's elegiac strain
Steal o'er the heart,—and with a sense refin'd
    Of calm enjoyment, o'er each feeling reign:
    And thus from age to age shall they remain,
Alike to youth and hoary wisdom dear.   .
    Oh! what compar'd with these, can man obtain
From all the triumphs of that proud career,
By which the warrior trusts his monument to rear.

Survey mankind,—and say if there be aught
    In all their schemes and their ambitious views,
More worthy of a mind by wisdom taught,
    Than are the labours of the virtuous muse:
    Oh! who would fashion or ambition choose,
'To guide his steps thro' life's bewildering maze,
    If in his heart the minstrel might infuse
That taste for wisdom and for virtue's ways,
Which lift above the crowd, its censure and its praise.

'Tho' such the minstrel's aim, he fears this verse
    May prove unworthy of the high design,
The charms of truth and virtue to rehearse,
    The heart to soften, and the soul refine;
    Yet does he not affect with those to shine,
The mighty masters of the tuneful art;
    Content, if in his verse some touching line
A love for nature and for truth impart,
Or feed devotion's flame, within the youthful heart.
    Occoquan, Va. 1838.

THE LAST OF THE LENAPÉ.

The incidents in this poem were related to the author by his valued friend Dr. Joseph Parrish, of Philadelphia, who derived them from a tradition preserved in his family. They took place about the year 1683.

PART I.

THE LANDING.

On Delaware's majestic stream
   A stately ship appears,
Around her bows the foaming spray
Is dashing, as upon her way
   With upward course she steers.

Upon her deck may you behold
   A group of pilgrims stand,
The old and young are gather'd there,
The matron and the maiden fair,
   A meek, devoted band.

With eager eyes they gaze around,
  This promis'd land to see,
To these lone solitudes they come,
To seek a peaceful quiet home,
  From persecution free.

Full well they know the Indian dwells
  In native wildness here;
But safe in God's protecting hand,
Who call'd them from their native land, .
  Their hearts are void of fear.

Oh! what emotions new and strange,
  Within their bosoms rise,
As yon dense forest, wild and green,
So different from the cultur'd scene
  Of Britain, meets their eyes.

They seem indeed transported now,
  To some far-distant sphere,
Yet the same sun does on them shine,
And the same beams of love Divine,
  Their lonely bosoms cheer.

Among that group a mother stands,
  Whose children, gather'd round,
A tender father's loss deplore,
Who, where the ocean billows roar,
  A watery grave has found.

Silent and sad, with grief absorb'd,
  Unconscious does she stand,
Her eyes the present scenes survey,
But ah! her thoughts are far away,
  In her dear native land.

She thinks of him forever dear,
  Whose home is now above,
But to her vision does he seem
As when in youth's delightful dream,
  Their hearts were joined in love.

For even then this distant clime,
  Had in their views become
Another Eden's blissful bower,
Where pure religion's sacred flower
  Should unmolested bloom.

Then did they hope this favour'd land
  Their future home would be,
Where life's pure stream would sweetly glide,
Until it mingled with the tide
  Of blest eternity.

But ah! how soon that dear support,
  From her embrace is wrung,
And like a tender vine, is she
Bereft of that protecting tree,
  To which she fondly clung.
   3*

Oh! lovely mourner, grieve not thus,
   Lift up thine eyes and see,—
Will not that Being who bestow'd
This beauteous land for man's abode,
   Protect and strengthen thee?

But now the ship that spot hath gain'd
   Beneath the pine trees shade,
Where, on the noble river's strand,
Penn's virgin city soon shall stand,
   In modest garb array'd.

" Oh! mother see! a warrior comes,"
   The wondering children cry:
With a proud step he seems to tread,—
Erect his form,—and o'er his head
   Are feathers waving high.

A hatchet in his belt he wears,
   Which has with blood been stained,
And now he launches on the tide,
And soon the gallant vessel's side
   His swift canoe has gain'd.

And on the lofty vessel's deck,
   Lenapé's chieftain springs,
He comes to welcome them ashore,
And venison a plenteous store
   In his canoe he brings.

He looks around, and soon espies
   The widow'd mother there,
And with a nice discernment blest,
He singles her from all the rest,
   For his protecting care.

" Daughter of Onas," said the chief,
   " Shed not the mournful tear,
By the Good Spirit am I sent,
And his the blessings I present,
   Thy lonely heart to cheer.

" What tho' no house nor wigwam yet
   Hath been prepar'd for thee;
Where yon high bank o'erlooks the wave,
There is a safe, secluded cave,
   Where thou mayest shelter'd be."

Conducted by their warrior guide,
   Within the cave they come;
And now from long confinement free,
The joyous children shout for glee,
   Delighted with their home.

As when a bird her nest would build,
   In some secure retreat,
Dry leaves and grass are strew'd within,
And at the door a leafy screen
   Shuts out the noon-day heat.

There, blest with piety and love,
  Their peaceful days are spent;
No baron in his palace home,
Nor king beneath his gilded dome,
  Is half so well content.

Oh! soul-sustaining piety,
  In mercy art thou given,
O'er every sea, man's bark to guide,
Whether with favouring gales supplied,
  Or by the tempest driven.

Whether in sunny climes becalm'd,
  Or wrapp'd in arctic gloom,
Thro' every scene canst thou sustain,
Until that final port we gain
  Where storms shall never come.

THE LAST OF THE LENAPÉ.

PART II.

THE FIRST WINTER.

The Indian summer now is past,
  The forest leaves are sear,
The fruits of autumn strew the ground,
And hollow winds, with dreary sound,
  Proclaim the winter near.

Within the cave the matron dwelt,
  Summer and autumn through;
Tho' oft her faith was sorely tried,
Yet still by Providence supplied
  With food in season due.

The Indian, faithful to his trust,
  His proffer'd word fulfill'd;
The " lone one" did he call her then,
And never once forgot her, when
  The antler'd deer he kill'd.

But sometimes fruitless was the chase
   Through forests drear and wide;
Then to the cave the generous chief
Could bring her children no relief,
   Nor for his own provide.

But o'er them still does Heavenly Love
   Extend his guardian care;
Above yon forests, waving high,
On rustling wings, the pidgeons fly,
   And darken all the air.

Like a vast cloud they settle down
   On every tree around,
As when in Israel's sore distress
Upon the lonely wilderness,
   The flock of quails was found.

Yet ah! how different from the meat
   To murmuring Israel given;
For that became their punishment,
While this to thankful hearts is sent,
   A gracious boon from heaven.

Now winter, riding on the blast,
   Comes wrapp'd in clouds and gloom,—
The laughing rills are hushed,—and all
The fairest plants of nature fall,
   Dismantled of their bloom.

Whence shall they now their food procure ?
   The feather'd flocks have flown,
The fish are in the frozen floods,
The deer are in the distant woods,
   And cattle they have none.

As thus, with gloomy thoughts oppress'd,
   Wears on the wintry day,—
While Christmas-eve is drawing near,
They think upon the joyous cheer
   Of Britain, far away.

Transported to that distant scene
   By fancy's magic power,
They hear the greeting of their friends,
And see the gladness that attends
   The happy evening hour.

But soon their wandering thoughts, call'd home,
   Those genial scenes must leave;
No kindred greetings do they hear,
Nor have they aught of joyous cheer,
   To glad the lingering eve.

Let not your hearts in grief despond,
   A guardian Power is nigh;
For he who gives the sparrows food,
And watches o'er the raven's brood,
   Will hear the orphan's cry.

Hark now! that trampling thro' the snow!
   Your Indian friend has come;
Laden with venison and corn,
And berries from the forests borne,
   He seeks the widow's home.

"Daughter of Onas," said the chief,
   " God has been good to me;
He blest me while I sought for game,
And this, which from his bounty came,
   He bade me bring to thee."

With gratitude they welcome in
   The generous-hearted chief;
But, most of all, they bless that Power
Who sent them, in the needful hour,
   Such opportune relief.

Thus did the heavenly Father's care
   Their fainting hearts sustain,
And shield them from the wintry blast,
Until the gladsome spring, at last
   Came smiling o'er the plain.

Oh! Heavenly Love! while in our hearts,
   Thy righteous sceptre sways,
In desert plains will fountains spring,
And cause the lonely heart to sing,
   With gratitude and praise.

" Beauty for ashes," dost thou give,
    "'The oil of joy for woe,"
The darkest hours canst thou illume,
And cause the wilderness to bloom
    A paradise below.

4

THE LAST OF THE LENAPÉ.

PART III.

THE CONCLUSION.

FROM groves array'd in vernal green
  The notes of joy resound,
The grass puts forth,—the wild flowers spring,—
And orchard trees are blossoming,
  In gay profusion round.

The widow'd mother now comes forth,
  And leaves her lone retreat;
A friend who sought the ocean wave,
To her his humble dwelling gave,
  A cottage fair and neat.

With cheerful hearts, her duteous sons
  Their rural tasks assume;
The fruitful fields with care they till,
And garden spot,—whose roses fill
  The air with sweet perfume.

In rural labours crown'd with peace,
　　Their prosperous lives were spent;
For while with care they till'd their lands,
To grateful hearts, and willing hands,
　　Were fruitful seasons sent.

Their race a noble tree became,
　　Enrich'd with golden fruit;
Its branches were extended wide,
For filial piety supplied
　　The nurture of its root.

But where is he, who that fair tree,
　　Protected while it rose,—
Does he partake its fruit mature?
Or in declining life, secure,
　　Beneath its shade repose?

Yes, still within their grateful hearts
　　The Indian's name was dear:
They sought his wigwam distant far,
And friendship's bright, benignant star,
　　His evening hour did cheer.

His memory too was handed down
　　From grateful sire to son;
But like the frost in morning's ray,
So did his tribe all melt away,
　　Till there was left,—but one.

That one,—sad relic of a tribe,
  Now pass'd from earth away,
They brought to their own home,—and there
They cherish'd her with pious care
  Till life's last closing day.

Where Brandywine rolls sweetly by,
  Is her last resting place;
And wild flowers now are blooming round,
To mark the sole memorial found
  Of that departed race.

And oft at evening's pensive hour,
  In thoughtful mood reclined,
While musing on those scenes long past,
We feel their deep'ning shadows cast
  A sadness o'er the mind.

The lofty forest trees are gone
  From Schuylkill's rocky shore;
But ah! a nobler race than they
From Penn's fair land has pass'd away,
  And shall return no more.

Some rooted up,—and some by force
  Transplanted far away:
Like oaks whose blasted tops are dead,
And all their leafy honours shed
  In premature decay.

Children of Onas! do they not
  Deserve our fostering aid?
Our father's, once a feeble band,
While strangers in a foreign land,
  Repos'd beneath their shade,

4*

NOTES.

IT is stated in *Watson's Annals of Philadelphia*, that the tribe of Indians first found about the regions of the river Delaware, and thence called the Delawares, never used that name among themselves; they called themselves *Lenni Lenape*, which means "the original people"—Lenni, meaning "original."

Page 24—verse 2nd.

"Full well they know the Indian dwells
In native wildness here."

Richard Townsend in his "Testimony showing the providential hand of God to him and others, from the first settlement of Pennsylvania to this day," (about the year 1727,) thus speaks of the Indians:

"At our arrival (1682) we found it a wilderness; the chief inhabitants were Indians, and some Swedes, who received us in a friendly manner,—and though there was a great number of us, the good hand of Providence was seen in a particular manner, in that provisions were found for us by the Swedes and Indians, at very reasonable rates, as well as brought from divers other parts that were inhabited before. And as our worthy proprietor treated the Indians with extraordinary humanity, they became very civil and loving to us, and brought in abundance of venison. As in other countries, the Indians were exasperated by hard treatment, which hath been the foundation of much bloodshed, so the contrary treatment hath produced their love and affection."—*Proud's History*, vol. 1, page 229.

Page 24—verse 2nd.

"But safe in God's protecting hand,
Who call'd them from their native land,
Their hearts are void of fear."

It appears that many of the first settlers of this colony, consi‌dered themselves called to the undertaking by higher motives than merely to better their temporal condition. William Penn thus speaks of his own motives. "I eye the Lord in the obtaining the country; and as I have so obtained, I desire I may not be unworthy of his love, but do that which may answer his kind providence and serve his truth and people, that an example may be set up to the nations. There may be room there though not here (in England) for such an holy experiment."—*Watson's Annals*, page 60.

Richard Townsend says, "Our *first concern* was to keep up and maintain our *religious worship*, and in order thereunto, we had several meetings in the houses of the inhabitants; and one boarded meeting house was set up where the city was to be, near Delaware, and as we had nothing but love and good-will in our hearts, one to another, we had very comfortable meetings, from time to time; and after our meetings were over, we assisted each other in building houses for our shelter."—*Proud's History*, vol. 1.

Page 24—verse 5th.

"Among that group a mother stands."

The mother here alluded to was Hannah Chandler, who lost her husband on the passage, and being left with ten small children, she arrived at the colony in much distress, but was kindly provided for by the Indians.

Some of the same incidents are related in *Watson's Annals*, page 70.

Page 26—verse 2nd.

" But now the ship that spot hath gain'd
Beneath the pine trees shade,
Where, on the noble river's strand,
Penn's virgin city soon shall stand,
In modest garb array'd."

The spot where Philadelphia now stands, fronting on the Delaware, was at the time of its settlement, a high bank covered with lofty pines. In this bank some of the first colonists excavated caves for a temporary residence, until they could erect dwellings. Some of these caves remained for a long time, and a full account of them may be seen in *Watson's Annals*, page 159. They are also mentioned in *Proud's History*, vol. 1, page 225.

Penn's "virgin city" is thus spoken of by her founder in a valedictory letter to his friends, written in 1684, from on board the ship on his departure for England. "And thou Philadelphia, the virgin settlement of this province, named before thou wert born, what love, what care, what service, and what travail, has there been to bring thee forth, and preserve thee from such as would abuse and defile thee. Oh! that thou mayst be kept from the evil that would overwhelm thee; that, faithful to the God of thy mercies, in the life of righteousness, thou mayst be preserved to the end: my soul prays to God for thee, that thou mayst stand in the day of trial, that thy children may be blessed of the Lord, and thy people saved by his power; my love to thee has been great, and the remembrance of thee affects mine heart and mine eye! The God of eternal strength keep and preserve thee, to his glory and thy peace."—*Proud's History*, vol. 1.

Page 27—verse 2nd.

"Daughter of Onas, said the chief."

H. St. John, in his description of Pennsylvania, thus speaks of the name given by the Indians to William Penn: "He treated the natives like brothers, and these natives forgetting their ferocity and the hatred they bore to all Europeans, have never ceased to love and respect the Friends. They gave to Penn the name of Onas, (father) which some of their principal chiefs also bear to this day."

Page 28—verse 1st.

"No baron in his palace home,
Nor king beneath his gilded dome,
Is half so well content."

This stanza sounds to the *author* like an imitation of something he has read, but he cannot tell where. It is very possible that a near resemblance or coincidence of ideas may sometimes occur in different authors, where there is no intention of borrowing without due acknowledgement from the productions of others. So large a portion of our knowledge is necessarily derived from reading, that we may unconsciously at times adopt the ideas of others, without being able to tell from whence they were derived.

Page 29—verse 3rd.

"The 'lone one' did he call her then."

This title given by the Indians to Hannah Chandler, has been handed down by tradition amongst her descendants.

Page 30—verse 2nd.

"Above yon forests, waving high,
On rustling wings, the pidgeons fly,
And darken all the air."

So rapid was the settlement of this province that they must have suffered greatly for provisions, had they not been relieved at times by the immense flocks of *wild pidgeons.* "They came in such numbers that the air was sometimes darkened by their flight; and flying low they were frequently knocked down as they flew, in great quantities, by those who had no other means to take them, whereby they supplied themselves; and having salted those which they could not immediately use, they preserved them both for *bread and meat.*"—*Proud's History,* vol. 1, page 223.

Page 35—verse 5th.

" But like the frost in morning's ray,
So did his tribe all melt away,
Till there was left—but one."

The "Last of the Lenapé," nearest resident to Philadelphia, died in Chester county, in the person of "Old Indian Hannah," in 1803. She had her wigwam many years upon the Brandywine, and used to travel much about in selling her baskets, &c.; on such occasions, she was often followed by her dog and her pigs, all stopping where she did. She lived to be nearly one hundred years of age—had a proud and lofty spirit to the last—hated the blacks, and scarcely brooked the lower orders of the whites. Her family before her, had dwelt with other Indians in Kennett township.— She often spoke emphatically of the wrongs and misfortunes of her race, upon whom her affections still dwelt. As she grew old, she quitted her solitude, and dwelt in friendly families.—*Watson's Annals*, page 447.

In addition to this information, I have been told that the families who took care of this last of her tribe, were descendants of Hannah Chandler, who had been so signally befriended by the Indians. They buried her near the forks of the Brandywine, in an Indian burying ground, distant eleven miles from the place where she died.

TEWINISSA.*

PART I.

THE LOST CHILD.

WHERE swift Esopus pours his flood
    Beside the mountains blue,
Lefever's modest mansion stood,
    By forests hid from view.

* The incidents related in this Poem, are derived from a letter
of H. St. John de Crevecoeur, written from Carlisle, in Pennsyl-
vania, in 1773. He says he was an eye witness of the scene re-
lated, and was well acquainted with Lefever and Tewinissa.

It appears that Tewinissa lived at an Indian village, called Ana-
quaga, situated on the eastern side of the river Susquehanna, in
Pennsylvania. Lefever lived near the river Esopus, at the foot of
the Blue Ridge, in Ulster county, New York. He was the grand-
son of a Frenchman who was obliged to abandon his country at
the time of the revocation of the Edict of Nantes. The writer
above mentioned, who was well acquainted with the Indians, says
that the instance here related was the first time he ever knew one
to shed tears. He says the young Lefever, when he grew up to

5

'Twas in a valley, rich and fair,
    By hills encompass'd round,
And many a wolf and panther's lair
    Among their shades was found.

A wife belov'd, Lefever had,
    And children ten had they;
The youngest one, a prattling lad,
    Was beautiful and gay.

Like evening's last and loveliest beam,
    This gift of heaven appears,
Dispensing gladness o'er the stream
    Of their departing years.

At eventide, replete with joy,
    How glide the hours away,
Whilst old Lefever and his boy
    Engage in mirthful play.

And when upon the grassy lawn
    Appear the dew-drops bright,
That boy is up at earliest dawn,
    And carols with delight.

manhood, never abandoned the name which was given him on this occasion. He signed his name Tewinissa Lefever; and he went to the Indian village and adopted as his brother, one of Tewinissa's sons, who bore the same name.

But o'er this scene, alas! too soon,
   Did clouds of sorrow come;
The child one summer day at noon
   Is missing from his home.

The parents search on every hand,
   And neighbours kindly aid,
Thro' field and forest spread the band,
   And thro' the mountain glade.

Meanwhile the parents moan and grieve,
   And call their boy in vain,
Until the darksome shades of eve,
   Come stealing o'er the plain.

Alas! the sorrowing parents say,
   Our darling boy is gone;
On him will wolves or panthers prey,
   Before the morning's dawn.

And thus the lingering hours are past,
   Throughout the livelong night,
Each hour seems darker than the last,
   From eve till morning's light.

And when the morning's light is come,
   No tidings do they hear;
And dark and dreary is their home,
   Bereft of one so dear.

But now an Indian's form they see,
   Forth from the forest glide,
A large and faithful dog has he,
   That frolics by his side.

Towards Lefever's house he came,
   And sought his friendly door;
And Tewinissa was the name
   The welcome stranger bore.

He sees the parents' deep distress,
   And hears them vainly mourn;
"Go bring to me," the Indian says,
   "A shoe the boy has worn."

He tells his dog to smell the shoe,
   And seek the infant's trail;
The dog looks up as tho' he knew,
   And felt the mournful tale.

And now they take a circuit round,
   To seek the absent boy,
And soon the dog his trail has found,
   And barking, springs for joy.

Away they went thro' field and wood,
   Their hearts were fill'd with glee,
And soon beside the child they stood,
   Beneath a spreading tree.

There did he lie,—and safe from harm,
  By gentle sleep o'ercome;
The Indian laid him on his arm,
  And softly bore him home.

What transport fill'd the father's breast,
  The mother wept for joy;
The Indian to their hearts they press'd,
  And kiss'd their darling boy.

" What shall I give," the father said,
  "To recompense thy care?"
The Indian turn'd away his head,
  To hide a starting tear.

Then in his native lustre shone,
  The red man wild and free;
" Thy wealth," he said, " I would not own,
  Nor wages take from thee.

"Give me thy hand,—and when we part,
  Think of me while away;
None but the treasures of the heart,
  For works of love can pay."

" Oh, let me then thy kindred claim,
  My brother thou shalt be;
I'll call this boy by thy dear name,
  And may he be like thee."

  5*

Parental love! how dost thou fill
   Our hearts with joy or woe;
Thy throb of grief,—thy joyful thrill,
   Can parents only know.

In his impetuous, wild career,
   The thoughtless youth may rove,
Nor heed a father's watchful care,
   Nor prize a mother's love.

But when he comes, in after years,
   To act the parent's part,
He knows the hopes and anxious fears
   That fill a father's heart.

And oh! if death before that day,
   His parents should remove,
How shall he then the debt repay,
   Of all their care and love.

May then each dear ingenuous youth,
   To heaven direct his prayer,
A tender mother's heart to soothe,
   And bless a father's care.

TEWINISSA.

PART II.

THE BROTHERS.

His neighbours now are gather'd round
   Lefever's festive board;
There Tewinissa too is found,
   And there the boy restor'd.

" Behold, my friends and neighbours dear,"
   'Twas thus Lefever spake,
" I call on you to witness here,
   The covenant I make.

" Henceforth my brother, by thy name
   This boy shall be address'd;
And by this wampum's sacred claim,
   I bind thee to my breast.

" My wife and I the staff deplor'd,
  Of our declining years;
Thou hast to us that staff restor'd,
  And dried our flowing tears.

" Should dark affliction o'er thy home,
  A wintry tempest bring,
Then mayst thou here, my brother, come,
  And find the bloom of spring.

" For here affection's flowers shall be,
  Their sweets diffusing round;
A wigwam will I build for thee,
  On thy own native ground.

" No land do I presume to give,
  Thy wanderings to restrain,
For here did thy forefathers live,
  And here mayst thou remain.

" Shouldst thou or sick or wounded be,
  My aid will I impart,
For thou hast been a friend to me,
  And heal'd my bleeding heart.

" And when thy faithful dog no more
  Can chase the fleeting deer,
Then let him seek Lefever's door,
  And find a shelter here.''

While thus the good Lefever spoke,
  His friends admiring stood;
At length the Indian silence broke,
  And thus the theme pursued.

" Brother ! thy belt of wampum hath
  Fast bound this heart of mine,
And with its folds I sweep the path,
  Between my home and thine.

" What tho' of different blood we be,
  My fire has thine become;
Its smoke ascending thou shalt see,
  To guide thee to my home.

" Nought have I done thy heart to cheer,
  Thou wouldst not do for me;
'Twas the Good Spirit led me here,
  And his the praise should be.

" This wampum now, my brother, take,
  And hand it to thy boy,
And may our sons like us partake
  The pipe of peace and joy."

Such was the league contracted then,
  Between these friends so true,
And like the treaty made with Penn,
  Forever kept in view.

The scene has changed,—too bright to last
　　While months and years roll'd o'er;
The good Lefever too has past,
　　To an eternal shore.

And now the aged Indian lies
　　On his expiring bed;
To him the young Lefever flies,
　　By love and duty led.

" I come," he says, " to urge my claim
　　Fraternal to thy son,
We both have borne thy honour'd name,
　　Then may our hearts be one.

" Existence do I owe to thee,
　　For thou my life didst save,
Then let thy son my brother be,
　　When thou art in the grave."

For them the pious Indian sent
　　To heaven his last request,
Then calmly clos'd his eyes, and went
　　To his eternal rest.

Oh! love fraternal! seldom met
　　On earth so pure as this,
How dost thou soften each regret,
　　And sweeten every bliss.

When back we look o'er pleasures past,
   As from some rising ground,
The pausing traveller would cast
   His eyes on scenes around;

How bright to memory's view appear,
   Those spots forever green;
Where brothers kind and sisters dear,
   Around our paths have been.

Oh! scenes of youthful happiness,
   While hearts were warm and true,
When sorrows come and cares oppress,
   We sigh, and think of you.

Who thus at noon of life can stand,
   And backward cast his gaze,
Nor miss some member of a band,
   Beloved in early days.

Some friend in whom his heart repos'd,
   Has run his brief career;
The grave has o'er a brother clos'd,
   Or youthful sister dear.

By all the joys that once have been,
   And all the ties of love,
They call us from the present scene,
   And fix our thoughts above.

Tho' days of storm and nights of gloom,
  May blight our prospects here,
The flowers of virtue ever bloom,
  In that eternal sphere.

TEWINISSA.

PART III.

THE APPEAL.

Oh! where is now that mighty band,
    Who liv'd in days of yore,
Who met our fathers on the strand,
    And welcom'd them ashore.

Who roam'd the trackless wild for meat,
    Their hunger to appease,
Who spread for them the fur-clad seat,
    And brought the pipe of peace.

Alas! those hearts so kind and true,
    Have found their final rest,
And their descendants, weak and few,
    Are in the distant west.

6

The tide of emigration, strong
 As ocean's rolling waves,
Still bears their shatter'd barks along,
 Far from their fathers' graves.

Shall not my countrymen awake,
 And stop this sad career?
Are there no hearts for mercy's sake,
 To pour the pitying tear?

No friendly arm does there remain,
 That feeble band to save?
Alas! the lust of power and gain,
 Have mark'd them for the grave.

Now like the partridge on the hills,
 They change their place in vain;
Or like the deer the huntsman kills,
 Unpitied are they slain.

In vain for them, to hearts of steel
 We urge our earnest prayer;
Oh! let us then to you appeal,
 The young,—the good,—the fair.

If broken faith, and honour stain'd,
 And violated laws,
Your generous hearts have griev'd and pain'd,
 Stand forth and plead their cause.

Not as the world for suffering pleads,
　　Opposing force to force,
But as the meek Redeemer leads
　　In mercy's gentle course.

For oh! the cries of their distress
　　May even yet be heard,
If urged by youthful tenderness,
　　And love's persuasive word.

And let our prayers on high ascend,
　　His favour to secure,
Who is the homeless wanderer's friend,
　　And watches o'er the poor.

But oh! my country, where will be
　　Thy confidence and trust,
Should days of vengeance come to thee,
　　In retribution just.

May He who rules in power on high,
　　Avert that fatal day,
Teach thee to hear the mourner's sigh,
　　And wipe his tears away.

A NIGHT SCENE

AMONG THE MOUNTAINS OF VIRGINIA.

How calm and glorious is the hour of night,
  In these uncultur'd solitary wilds,
When o'er each lowly vale and lofty height,
  The full-orb'd moon in cloudless lustre smiles.

Those lofty mountains with their forests green,
  And craggy summits towering to the sky,
How proudly do they rise o'er all the scene,
  And lift the mind from earth to muse on high.

And yon pure rivulet that pours along,
  Playing and sparkling in the moonbeams clear,
How sweet the music of its vesper song,
  In changeful cadence falls upon the ear.

And hark! the roar of those far-spreading woods,
  Sinking or rising as the wind sweeps by;
Myriads of voices fill these solitudes,
  And send the notes of melody on high.

While all His works with one accord rejoice,
    And pour forth praises to the Great Supreme,
Shall man, unmov'd, withhold his nobler voice,
    Nor glow with rapture on the glorious theme.

His bounteous goodness all creation fills,
    Even these wild woods where solitude prevails,
He sends his dews upon the untrodden hills,
    And flowers he scatters o'er the lonely vales.

Scenes unfrequented by the feet of men,
    Display his goodness and proclaim his might;
He feeds the wild deer in the secret glen,
    And the young eagles on the craggy height.

His mighty hand the vivid lightning speeds,
    And bursts the clouds that o'er the hills impend:
The mountain stream thro' distant lands he leads,
    While joy and melody his steps attend.

To trace his wonders thro' each varying clime,
    And all his mercies to the sons of men,
Fills the rapt soul with ecstasy sublime,
    Beyond the efforts of the poet's pen.

Oh! solitude, how blissful are the hours,
    Among thy shades in heavenly musing past,
When nature leads us thro' her secret bowers,
    And contemplation spreads the rich repast.
    6*

Among the haunts of men, the thoughtful mind
   That fain would rise above the things of earth,
Finds her bold flights on every hand confin'd,
   By care distracted, and seduc'd by mirth.

But in the deep and solemn hour of night,
   The soul luxuriates in a scene like this,
From cliff to cliff she wings her daring flight,
   O'er foaming cataract, or dark abyss.*

Or else, uplifted o'er the things of time,
   By heavenly faith from all her bonds set free,
Among the fields of ether soars sublime,
   And holds communion with the Deity.

Oh! how transporting is the glorious thought,
   That He, whose power upholds yon worlds above,
Is ever nigh, and ever found when sought,
   To save and bless us with a father's love.

Even His chastisements are with mercy fraught,
   And seal instruction on the attentive mind;
Driven by disease, these distant shades I sought,
   And all the fruitless cares of life resign'd.

   * See Chataubriand's description of a night spent in the deserts of the new world. He says, "In this wilderness the soul is delighted to plunge into an ocean of forests, to wander on the brink of immense lakes, to hover over the gulf of cataracts, and if I may so express myself, to find itself alone in the presence of the Deity."

'Twas then He met me, and in mercy heal'd
　The raging fever that my strength depress'd;
His love paternal to my soul reveal'd,
　And swell'd the tide of rapture in my breast.

Then oh! my soul, mayst thou continual turn,
　To Him whose power alone can guide thy ways,
May love divine upon thy altar burn,
　And every thought and feeling speak His praise.
　　1829.

THE COUNTRY SCHOOL HOUSE.

(A PRIZE POEM.)

NEAR yonder oak that rears its blasted head,
   Its aged trunk with verdant moss o'ergrown,
A School House stood, (that day long since has fled,)
   Where many an hour of blissful youth I've known.

It was a lovely spot as e'er was found,
   By nature form'd t' inspire the heart of youth;
There science might indulge in thought profound,
   Or contemplation soar to heavenly truth.

A little lonely glen with flow'rets sown,
   Whose mingled sweets the passing winds inhale,
A crystal stream with alder shrubs o'ergrown,
   Meandering slowly, wanders thro' the vale.

While all around the mighty forests rise,
   Where nature's choir continual concert keep,
And towering hills whose heads invade the skies,
   And frowning rocks and precipices steep.

When first the east was streak'd with rosy red,
　　And bright Aurora usher'd in the day,
Towards this spot have Edwin's comrades sped,
　　While he reluctant, linger'd by the way.

Sometimes he wandered thro' the shady wood,
　　To hear the red-bird's fascinating lay,
Or hung enraptur'd o'er the crystal flood,
　　Beneath whose waves the sportive sun-fish play.

Or else, perhaps, more pleasing still, I trust,
　　He roved delighted with some youthful fair,
Or sought the fountain to assuage her thirst,
　　Or plucked the wild-rose to adorn her hair.

Oh! who has felt the glow of early love,
　　And in the dimpling smile discern'd his fate,
Feels not wherever after he may rove,
　　This was to him an Eden's blissful state.

Oh! who has roam'd in rural scenes like this,
　　Where nature's choir the joyful anthem pour,
Nor tasted aught of more than earthly bliss,
　　Nor felt his soul to thoughts sublimer soar.

It is the glow of youthful fire that lives,
　　And sheds its influence thro' the rural train,
And the blest charm of innocence, that gives
　　Increas'd luxuriance to the flowery plain.

Oh! heaven-born Innocence, extend thy reign,
  And may thy charms still more our hearts engage;
Compar'd with thee what are the fruits of gain,
  Or laurel wreaths that prompt the warrior's rage.

Not all the praise on history's page enroll'd,
  Can stay the course of man's expiring breath,
Nor fame's loud trump, nor ramparts form'd of gold,
  Control the ravage of the victor, death.

Oh! no, 'tis heavenly truth alone can shed,
  , Round man a glory that shall never fade;
It forms a halo round the christian's head,
  That lights his passage thro' death's dreary shade.

The school-boy's heart when roving thro' these fields,
  To fame's report, and honour's voice unknown,
More lasting bliss, more true enjoyment yields,
  Than does ambition seated on a throne.

Down in the vale where morning's shades repose,
  Young Edwin sees the school house rise to view,
Thither with listless, loitering steps, he goes
  The dull routine of study to pursue.

Oh! how they watch the slow ascending sun
  Climb thro' the azure of the vaulted sky;
And when one half his daily course is run,
  To rural sports the longing urchins fly.

Some now are seen to heave the whirling quoit,
   Or throw the bounding ball with nervous strength;
Some thro' the woods pursue a comrade's flight,
   And 'neath the shade some lie at listless length.

But soon, obedient to the teacher's call,
   Back to the school they slowly wend their way,
Reluctant leave the chase, the quoit, the ball,
   And sylvan shade that seems to court their stay.

Dull flow the hours of painful durance there,
   While Edwin plies his task, or seems to ply,
Or steals the modest glance of maiden fair,
   Or views with anxious gaze the master's eye.

And when the sun, low verging to the west,
   Casts the long shades of evening o'er the plain,
With joy they hear once more the kind behest,
   That calls to blissful liberty again.

With many a gambol now they homeward go,
   And tell some tale of wonder by the way—
Or loitering, linger where the wild-flowers blow,
   Or watch the glories of departing day.

Where are ye now, my friends of former times,
   Where now ye kindred souls I held so dear;
Some gone methinks to other distant climes,
   And some perchance have clos'd life's short career.

Like kindred drops, then flowing side by side,
 We seem'd as destin'd not on earth to sever,
But soon some rock disparts affection's tide,
 And separates our friendly course forever.

Eve's sable curtains now are closing round,
 A few faint stars display their glimmering light;
The whip-poor-will with solitary sound,
 Recalls my thoughts from scenes of past delight.

The flaming sun has slowly sunk to rest,
 And yields the empire to the sable night,
But leaves the world, in yonder glowing west,
 The mild refraction of his lingering light.

Thus youth's bright flame must vanish from my view,
 And leave the gloom of darksome age behind,
But memory shall those blissful scenes renew,
 And shed its radiance o'er the glowing mind.

The moon with borrowed splendour thron'd on high,
 Softens the shadows of approaching even,
While not a cloud that meets the gazing eye,
 Disturbs the mild serenity of heaven.

Oh! may the close of my expiring day,
 Be as unclouded and as calm as this;
O'er it may hope, with mildly beaming ray,
 Reflect the sunshine of eternal bliss.
  1822.

POTOMAC.

Potomac! how I love at eve
   Upon thy pebbly shore to stand,
And see thy billows gently heave,
   And roll and break upon the strand.

There is a pensive feeling wrought
   By each successive solemn swell,
And many a long-lost, tender thought,
   Comes thronging forth from memory's cell.

Raised by the zephyr's gentle force,
   Thy billows roll towards the shore,
How beautiful, but short their course,—
   They break—and now are seen no more.

My bosom too has often heav'd,
  Potomac! like thy wavy breast,
With hopes and joys, I once believ'd
   Would flow till life should sink to rest;

7

Call'd up by one whose radiant eye
   Beam'd with intelligence and power,
Yet mild as zephyr's gentlest sigh,
   When breath'd upon an opening flower.

But ah! how short a course had they,
   Arrested soon by grief and pain,—
She like a zephyr pass'd away,
   And how shall they arise again!

Potomac! how I love, alone
   And pensive by thy shores to stray,
When day's refulgent blaze is gone,
   And moonbeams on thy waters play.

To see the queen of night ascend,
   With fleecy clouds around her furl'd,
Whilst yon bright sentinels attend,
   As if to guard a slumbering world.

The far receding hills appear
   An undulating streak of green;
And from the watery surface clear,
   Reflected, smiles the beauteous scene.

All,—all, is silent, save the sigh
   Of night winds sweeping o'er the deep,
Softly the murmuring waves reply,
   And then again are hush'd in sleep.

From such a noble scene, how springs
  On rapture's wing th' ethereal mind,
Spurns every thought of earthly things,
  And leaves her groveling cares behind.

She mounts from radiant sphere to sphere,
  From all the bonds of earth set free,
And feels His vital spirit near,
  Whose presence fills infinity.

   1824-5.

JEFFERSON'S ROCK,

AT HARPER'S FERRY, VA.

"It is worth a voyage across the Atlantic to see these monuments of a war between rivers and mountains, that must have shaken the earth to its centre."—*Jefferson's Notes on Virginia.*

FROM this huge rock high o'er the adjacent lands,
   How grand the scenes that round us rise to view;
So vast the prospect hence the eye commands,
   The name of Jefferson is justly due.

While on the south the Shenandoah laves
   The mountain's base, o'erhung with tufted woods,
Down from the west, Potomac's rolling waves
   Impetuous rush to meet their kindred floods.

They meet like allies, flush'd with warlike pride,
   And rush together on their mountain foe;
The mountain severs,—thro' the chasm wide,
   Tumbling and roaring, down the torrents flow.

How fancy loves on pinions unconfin'd
   Back o'er departed years to roam afar,
When first these streams their mighty forces join'd,
   And shook the globe with elemental war.

Her magic pencil paints the scene full bright,
   The circling whirlpool and the cascades bound,
Stupendous cliffs, hurled from their mountain height,
   And tumbling headlong, shake the forests round.

Then cleft asunder was the mountain's side,
   The raging floods then rush'd resistless through,
Thence rolling on spread devastation wide,
   Till awe-struck ocean from his shores withdrew.

To yonder cliffs now lift the excursive eye,—
   Sublimely grand appears the mountain scene:
See rocks on rocks gigantic pil'd on high,
   With laurels crown'd and forests waving green.

While far beneath, torn from their giddy steep,
   The mighty fragments of the cliffs we see,
O'er which the foaming waves continual sweep,
   And roaring, seem to tell their victory.

'Mid scenes like these, with what delight we view
   Far in the east, between the opening hills,
The clear horizon's placid azure hue,
   Which with a heavenly calm the bosom fills.

7 *

So feels the mind when on the brink of time,
  O'er life's tumultuous waves, uplifted high,
Some heavenly view of future bliss sublime,
  Transports the soul and cheers the mental eye.

From these grand views which every sense o'erpower,
  And hold the mind in vacant wonder's sway,
Well pleas'd I turn to yonder rural bower,
  Whose smiling site invites the traveller's stay.

Thick round its sides the clustering vines are hung,
  Abrupt the mountain rises in its rear,
Half hid by trees, the river glides along,
  And murmuring softly, soothes the listening ear.

Stupendous scenes, like splendour, wealth and power,
  To which mankind with eager grasp aspire,
'Tho' they may please for one short fleeting hour,
  Their brilliancy itself, at length will tire.

Then seeks the soul some calm, some blest retreat,
  Where milder beauties may forever please;
Thus Washington, from his exalted seat,
  Retir'd, and found tranquillity and ease.

How vast the wisdom then these scenes may teach,
  Of Him who call'd existence into day;
Few men the heights of fame can ever reach,
  But all may find an humbler, happier way.

Oh! Fame, thou dear, thou soul-deluding sound,
    Parent of care, and banisher of rest,
How many seek thee, but how few have found,
    And fewer still, in finding thee, are blest.

Even this same rock on which my feet are plac'd,
    Proves, clearly proves, how fondly thou art priz'd,—
Thick o'er its surface many a name is trac'd,
    And many a name that now forgotten lies.

How many a weary step some travellers climb
    O'er craggy rocks to reach this lovely place,
Almost forget to view those scenes sublime,
    And spend their time a worthless name to trace.

Like Macedon's young king renown'd afar,
    Whose bosom panted for the heights of fame,
For this he braved the iron-front of war,
    Attain'd the summit, and has left,—a name.

There is a deep, mysterious desire,
    By Heaven implanted in the human breast,
Which bids the soul to future life aspire,
    When in the grave this frame shall sink to rest.

When thoughts of death the human soul engage,
    And the pale messenger his form displays,
Who does not feel, like Rome's heroic sage,
    An ardent longing for immortal days.

When with celestial love this lights the soul,
  It then receives Religion's sacred name;
When worldly glory forms the inspiring goal,
  Its name on earth is then recorded Fame.

The first attun'd king David's hallowed lyre,
  While heavenly raptures flowing from his tongue,
Rais'd high the soul—and higher—and still higher—
  Till up to heaven the loud hosannas rung.

The other breathes in Homer's classic strain,
  And sheds its influence mild o'er Maro's lays,
Whose magic force while o'er each sense they reign,
  Calls forth the tribute of exalted praise.

As yon bright sun's declining beams now fade,
  The twilight gloom comes on with gradual pace;
The valleys first are 'velop'd in its shade,
  And now it climbs above the mountain's base.

But still yon cliffs that crown the lofty height,
  Give back the radiance of departing day,
And still shall shine in all their glory bright,
  'Till day's last lingering beam shall fade away.

So shall the brightest deeds of fame expire,
  And heroes' names be wrapped in death-like night;
But then, even then, shall David's hallowed lyre,
  Still wake its numbers in the realms of light.
    1822.

LAKE GEORGE.

Sweet, peaceful Lake! how would I love to glide
At morn and eve upon thy crystal tide ;
Push the light skiff along thy silent shore,
Where rocks and verdant woods are hanging o'er ;
Among the islands on thy bosom rove,
In shady nook or cool sequester'd grove ;
Or seek some cave beneath yon towering hill,
Where mossy rocks the crystal stream distil.
But not thro' scenes like these, alone, I'd stray,—
One dear companion still should cheer my way ;
Her brightening eye should on these beauties gaze,
Her raptur'd tongue should dwell upon their praise :
Meanwhile the stream of life would glide away,
Pure as thy waters, and serene as they.
   Oh ! I have watch'd with rapture-lighted eye
The earliest dawn that ting'd yon orient sky,—
Seen the blue mists around these mountains roll'd,
Their graceful outlines ting'd with burnish'd gold,
Till from yon cliffs that o'er the waters frown,
The sun, uprisen, pour'd his radiance down ;

Chas'd by his light, the sombre shades withdrew,
The scattered clouds in wild confusion flew,
Clear and distinct each beauteous scene became,
And all the mountain tops were fring'd with flame.
Delightful Lake! how grateful is the scene,
At sultry noon among thy islands green,
Where cool and shelter'd from the scorching ray,
The patient angler whiles the hours away;
Leans o'er the bank, and in the crystal tide
Sees round his hook the playful fishes glide,
Till some poor victim, tempted by the bait,
Is drawn reluctant to his hapless fate.
When o'er yon mountain glows the setting sun,
And all the labours of the day are done,
How would I love, devoid of care, to stray
Along thy shores, and watch the closing day,
See the last lingering beam of light that gilds
The craggy summits of yon eastern hills,
Or mark the shades of evening mantling round
Yon ancient fortress crumbling to the ground,
Where erst, the sons of men in wrathful hour,
Contended fiercely for the grasp of power:
But they who proudly met in that dread fray,
Shall meet and tremble on a greater day,
When all the power and all the fame they sought,
Weigh'd with Eternity, shall seem as naught.
Pure, peaceful Lake! long will my heart hold dear
The bright remembrance of the hours past here;

Where love's bright flame and friendship's genial ray
A pleasing radiance shed around my way,
And gave a lovelier form and brighter hue
To every scene that met my wondering view.

1826.

THE PEAKS OF OTTER.

Behold yon Peak with rocks gigantic crown'd,
And with a forest girdle circled round;
Its graceful outline swells before the eye,
In pleasing contrast with the azure sky;
And clothed in richest robes of living green,
It towers, the monarch of the mountain scene.
   Tho' years have flown, and joys and sorrows past
Have o'er my path their lights and shadows cast;
Yet memory still in vivid colours shows,
The glorious scene that on my vision rose,
When on that peak in musing solitude,
To watch the dawning of the day I stood.
First in the eastern sky those streaks of gray,
The blended hues of light and shade display;
Succeeded soon by tints of roseate dye,
Whose brightening radiance spreads along the sky;
And many a cloud attends in rich array,
To catch the glories of the rising day.
Far as the eye can reach, the prospect wide
With valleys, hills, and plains diversified,

Seen in the distance from this mountain height,
Like one vast plain is spread before the sight:
Where, seen at times and then conceal'd from view,
The glittering streams their winding course pursue,
And sleeping mists in every valley lie,
Like bright still lakes, deceptive to the eye.
But see! the rising sun with splendour glows,
The mists, awaken'd from their deep repose,
In graceful shapes their changeful forms display!
Then take the morning's wings and soar away;
What beauteous colours burst upon the sight,
Caught and reflected from the orb of light,
By whose bright beams uplifted, they appear
To rise triumphant to a higher sphere.

  Does not yon glorious orb an emblem seem
Of that eternal and life giving Beam,
Which from the soul can chase the gloom of night,
Refine and clothe it with a robe of light,
Endow with feelings of celestial birth,
And bear triumphant o'er the things of earth!

  As westward now we turn our wondering view
O'er yon wide-scatter'd hills and mountains blue;
We see the shadow of this lofty cone,
O'er many a distant ridge distinctly thrown,
Whose long-extended lines and graceful sweep,
Seem like the billows of the rolling deep.

  Oh! who on such a scene as this can gaze,
Nor feel his bosom glow with grateful praise
  8

To Him whose potent voice the word but said,
And mountains started from their ocean bed.
And oh! my country when I thus behold
Thy wide-extended plains, and mountains bold,
Thy vales secluded, thy embow'ring woods,
Thy rivers rolling their majestic floods,
Thy mighty cataract's unrivall'd scene,
And thy broad lakes that spread their waves serene,—
I feel the greatness of thy destiny,
And breathe to heaven the fervent prayer for thee,
That like thy scenery may thy virtues shine,
And bear the impress of a stamp divine.

    1838.

TO SERENA.

Oh! why, Serena, dost thou wear,
  So frequent on thy placid brow,
That sweetly musing pensive air,
      That clothes it now?

Methinks in many a lonely hour,
  The fading charms of earth resign'd,
Thou find'st in contemplation's bower,
      Joys more refin'd.

When worldly cares, and scenes of mirth,
  And all the fleeting dreams of life,
Whose influence binds us down to earth,
      Have ceas'd their strife,—

Thou know'st 'tis then the unfetter'd soul,
  Enraptur'd, seeks the " world of mind,"
And spurning earth's severe control,
      Soars unconfin'd,

'Tis then we find this speck of earth
    Was never destin'd to confine
A soul that claims a heavenly birth,—
      A spark divine.

Hast thou not thought in hours like this,
    How strange that mortals should forego,
The only lasting source of bliss,
      And balm of woe?

To sport awhile on pleasure's stream,
    To breathe of flattery's pois'nous breath,
And then from life's illusive dream
      Awake in death.

For me, all heedless as I am,
    A wanderer from the perfect way,
When restless Fancy finds a calm,
      These feelings sway.

Then looking back with heartfelt pain,
    Life's fleeting pleasures I review,
Repent, and say to Folly's train,
      Vain shades, adieu!

But ah! this vital spark, the mind,
    Is wedded to a frame of clay,
And all the follies, thus resign'd,
      Resume their sway.

Still then, Serena, may'st thou wear,
　　Forever on thy placid brow,
That sweetly musing, pensive air,
　　　　That clothes it now.

What tho' thy heart of purity,
　　Life's various follies hath resign'd,
Still mayst thou mourn—yes, mourn for me,
　　　　And all mankind.

Should some pure seraph from above,
　　A being of celestial birth,
Come down, a messenger of love,
　　　　And dwell on earth:

When he beheld th' afflictive scene,
　　The prostrate state of souls divine,
His brow, methinks, a pensive mien
　　　　Would wear like thine.

Alexandria, 1824.

8 *

SONNET TO A ROSE.

Sweet flower, that from the young Serena came,
   And in her bosom once thy fragrance shed,
   Tho' thy bright tints are now forever fled,
Still is the sweetness of thy scent the same.
Fit emblem thou, of that celestial flame,
   Which only in the virtuous bosom springs;
Whether affection or pure love its name,
   Dear are the cares, and sweet the joys it brings;
   Tho' time, dread spoiler of all earthly things,
May mar the beauty of the form it wears,
   The essence, still how faithfully it clings
   Around the heart, nor dreads the blight of years;
For with the soul, 'twill mount to higher spheres,
Improv'd in all its joys, and freed from all its cares.

SOMETHING NEW.

THERE is, methinks, beneath the sun
  (Whate'er the Jewish sage may say)
One object fair, and only one,
  That still is new from day to day.

Is it the bright kaleidoscope,
  That changes, turn it as you will?
Is it the rainbow, arch of hope,
  More beauteous and more changeful still?

Is it the cloud that veils the west,
  So gorgeously at summer even;
Which seems as tho' some spirit blest
  Were opening the gates of heaven?

Oh! no; it wears one constant hue,
  More bright than all of these can prove;
It is (I trust thou know'st it too)
  It is the holy flame of love.

The brightest things of earth will tire,
   Whate'er the charms they may display,—
The birds of spring, the minstrel's lyre,
   And e'en the cheering light of day.

But ah! there is in this a light,
   So clear, so constant, and so true;
From night till morn, and morn till night,
   We watch it, and it still is new.

AUTUMN.

A PASTORAL.

> "Of fellowship I speak
> Such as I seek, fit to participate
> All rational delight."
> MILTON.

AMELIA.

Oh! these are scenes that to the thoughtful mind
A language speak, which cannot be withstood,—
The varied foliage of autumnal groves,
The drooping flow'rets, and the leafless bowers,
From which yon little bird pours forth the notes
Of plaintive love, and chants his farewell song
To groves and bowers, the scenes of former bliss,
Ere he to other climes shall take his flight,
Where Summer, in the midst of Flora's train,
Delighted dwells, and calls the tuneful quire.

ALEXIS.

Yes, scenes like these are form'd to captivate
The feeling heart, and fill the thoughtful mind

With love of heavenly musing.   Thus the rose
That droops its lovely head, the leaf that falls
In graceful undulations to the earth,
The whispering evening breeze, green waving pines,
And murmuring brooks, all seem replete with life.
Chameleon-like, Imagination takes
Her changeful colours from the present scene,
And stamps their impress on the yielding heart.

    In hours like this she tells of life's decay,—
Of faded bowers of bliss,—and youthful hopes
Like vernal flowers, all wither'd,—brings to view
The objects dear of many a tender tie:
Friendships and former loves, like birds of spring,
Whose notes were wont to cheer,—remember'd still
With fond regret,—but ah! forever flown!
A thousand charms and soft endearing ties
Conspire to bind us to this lower world,
So fraught with bounteous gifts,—but were no trace
Of a supreme, creative mind, perceiv'd,
How dark would be the scene.   'Tis mind alone
That can commune with mind. Even the warm glance
And playful smile, and balmy lip of beauty,
If there no intellectual radiance shine,
How lifeless and how void.   Mark the young pair
That through yon grove of elms pursue their walk;
What beamy smiles and warm expressive looks
Evince the mutual interchange of thought.

AMELIA.

'Tis Edwin and Serena.   She the maid
Whose virtuous heart and highly cultur'd mind,
Have foremost plac'd among the village train;
The minstrel he, whose pleasing art calls forth
The purest aspirations of the soul.

ALEXIS.

Know'st thou the history of the youthful pair?

AMELIA.

Oh! it would take whole volumes to relate
The varied history of a mind impress'd
By nature's bounty, with a sense acute
Of suffering or enjoyment,—and on which
The lights and shades of life, alternately
Have fallen.   Suffice it then of him to say,
Three times has autumn held his sober reign,
Since Edwin's brow with clouds of grief o'erhung,
Bemoan'd the faded flowers of his green spring
By frosts untimely nipt.   Fond hopes were fled,
And schemes of bliss, indulg'd for many a year,
All blasted and decay'd.   He felt like one,
Who roaming through some house left desolate,—
Stripp'd of its furniture,—hears every step
Vibrate with hollow sound along the walls,
And strike a dreary chillness thro' the soul.
   He strove against these feelings, and put on

The garb of cheerfulness, to hide a heart
With anguish torn, and sought the giddy throng,
Where youth and beauty strove in vain, to chase
The secret sense of grief.   But there was one
Of modest mien, and pensive downcast eye,
And quiet spirit, cheerful yet not gay,
Who sometimes met him in the festive hall,
And gently drew him, with a cord unseen,
To shun the mirthful crowd.   There was a calm
And soothing influence in her placid looks,
That like the smile of innocence, could cheer
When mirth had tried in vain.   Such is the calm
That weary mortals prove,—when from the strife
And tumult of the day retir'd; comes on
The pensive twilight hour,—when not a cloud
Obscures the beauty of the blue serene,
And bright celestial orbs look down from high,
As if with nobler thoughts to inspire the soul.

  These interviews, repeated oft, he felt
A tender friendship in his bosom rise,
Like the soft radiance of the latter spring
When brightening into summer.   Then he sang
Upon his lyre, the virtues and the charms
Of young Serena,—but the modest fair
Discern'd not that for her was meant the strain,
And he unconscious that so much he lov'd,
Still thought no earthly fair should sway his heart,
The muse alone the mistress of his soul.

But there were seasons, when the muse no more
Could chase the gloom of care, or shed the light
Of gladness o'er his brow. Oh! then one smile
From those mild-beaming eyes, could more impart
Of heartfelt bliss, than poesy's bright dreams,
Or the sweet music of the world's applause.
This was a feeling different from the fire,
In youthful bosoms kindled, by the blaze
Of personal charms. Less wild and passionate,
But not less deep. The one like earth-born fires
That crown the summit of some lofty peak,—
Now bursting into flame,—now wrapt in gloom:
The other like pure Luna's milder beams,
Caught from the source of universal light,
And shedding beauty o'er the loneliest hours.
    At length he saw, or fondly thought he saw,
The sweet expression of a kind regard,
Which yet might brighten more and more,—and shed
A halo of pure light around two hearts,
Melted by love and blended into one.
But these warm raptures were succeeded oft
By trembling doubts and fears,—the maiden's worth
And his unworthiness contrasted, seem
All too unlike to meet. Such is the effect
In every mind where love triumphant reigns,
And many a valiant heart has fear'd to express,—
As he now fears,—the conflict in his breast.
    9

ALEXIS.

Oh! there is rapture in a flame like this!
We were not placed on earth to tread alone
This varied scene of mingled cares and joys.
But as yon beauteous moon our globe attends,
Through the long journey of a trackless sky;
Receiving each, and each dispensing light,
Drawn from one fountain of unceasing day,—
So man and woman were design'd to move
In beauteous concert thro' the path of life,
Enlightening and enlighten'd,—while they keep
In the bright orbit of celestial love.

SERENA.

A PASTORAL.

THE summer sun from his meridian height,
 On panting nature pours the sultry beam;
The winged warblers shun the blaze of light,
 And weary ploughmen loose the labouring team.
 Along the shore of Schuylkill's winding stream,
Where branching elms exclude the beams of day,
 Two youthful swains on many a pleasing theme,
In converse sweet, beguile the hours away;
And thus in soothing strains they raise the rural lay.

SIDNEY.

Oh! how refreshing is this sylvan shade,
 How sweet to hear yon brook run babbling by,
As on this grassy couch neglectful laid,
 With nature's charms we feast the roving eye,—
 Beyond the river's course yon mountains high,
In wild romantic ruggedness appear;
 And weeping willows on the shores we spy,

Which bend their boughs the murmuring floods to hear,
And birds amid those boughs, delight the listening ear.

And hark! the mocking bird's delightful note,
  With which the neighbouring grove melodious rings;
As thro' the air those strains so softly float,
  The passing zephyrs fold their downy wings:
  In Albion's clime, while Philomela sings,
The listening minstrel plans the warbler's praise,—
  But oh! ye bards, cease now to touch your strings,
A little while your boasted songstress stays,
While ours, for many a month, attunes her softer lays.

EDWIN.

And mark the contrast by yon river made,
  To all the smiling scenery around;
Along the windings of the peaceful glade,
  O'er rocks and crags it foams with roaring sound:
  Oh! Sidney, come, for wisdom's lore renown'd,
From nature's scenes instruct me to be good;
  Thy herds are grazing on the meadow ground,
And while my team partake their mid-day food,
I'll listen to thy lays, in this sequester'd wood.

SIDNEY.

'Tis not in learned lays, nor flowery strains
  To please the ear, that richest wisdom lies;

For humble David sooth'd a monarch's pains,
  While yet a youth in shepherd's homely guise:
  From deeper sources must those streams arise,
That yield instruction to th' immortal part;
  The babbling brook a summer's sun soon dries,
While fountains deep their waters still impart,
To save the fainting flocks, and cheer the shepherd's
    heart.

Though science is a mine, fraught with supplies
  Of richest ore, and gems of sparkling hues,
And literature a garden where the wise
  May gather plants for beauty and for use,—
  Yet how unwise is he who still pursues
Through life a path where only flowers are found;
  And how contracted are the miser's views,
With whom unpolish'd gems and ores abound,
Yet pines for lack of bread, while plenty smiles around.

'Tis not in hoarded heaps of richest ore
  The famish'd body can subsistence find,
Nor yet in idle uninstructive lore,
  To fill the cravings of th' immortal mind;
  But when with learning, goodness is combined,
Of brighter hues are fancy's flowers possess'd;
  The gold of science from its dross refin'd,
Is with a glorious image then impress'd—
Becomes a current coin, and makes us truly blest.
  9*

And oh! to souls like this alone is given
   That heart-felt rapture for the wise design'd,
To share at balmy morn or beauteous even,
   The smiles of nature, and the joys of mind;
   Nor will the sage despise that bliss refin'd,—
We sometimes feel our happiest moments stealing,
   When kindred souls by tender love entwin'd,
Unite in sacred sympathy of feeling;——
Oh! no: 'tis heaven's own law, the Maker's love re-
     vealing.

Bring not for us the tabor nor the lute,
   Nor sacred harp, attun'd with many a string,
Nor deep ton'd organ, nor melodious flute,
   To sing the praise of nature's bounteous king.
   A nobler instrument let christians bring,—
The heart itself, attun'd by skill divine,
   From whose soft tones far sweeter strains shall spring
Than when all these in artful concert join,
Where grand cathedral aisles the echoing notes confine.

The heart so form'd, where love's melodious strings,
   And christian faith, and hope, and joy are found,
Is like the harp of Æolus, which rings
   Whene'er the breath of heaven inspires the sound;
   Then oh! what sacred music wakes around,
Far sweeter than the fam'd Orphean lyre,
   Tho' mortal ears hear not the note profound,—

To heaven's high throne the grateful strains aspire,
And mingle with the praise of blest angelic choir.

EDWIN.

Oh! yes: and such the harmony that reigns
   In young Serena's pure unsullied mind,
When through the woodlands or the flowery plains
   With her I rove, what raptures do I find;
   I've sometimes thought a spirit so refin'd,
For some peculiar purpose must be given,
   With nobler views perhaps t' inspire mankind,
Or like the mildly beaming star of even,
In hours of doubt and gloom, to fix the thoughts on
     heaven.

     *   *   *   *   *   *

What gift, Serena, shall I bring for thee,
   Sweet to the ear and pleasing to the sight,—
Thou wouldst not wish the tuneful bird to see,
   Torn from his mate, depriv'd of nature's right,—
   Oh! no: for thee I'll climb the mountain height,
And pluck the wild flowers to adorn thy brow,—
   For thee the muse shall weave a garland bright,
And breathe in tender verse thy lover's vow;
For full of love, and truth, and tenderness art thou.

No childish fears Serena's bosom fill,—
   Too good, too pure, to dread the wrath of heaven:

As once with her I walk'd on yonder hill,
   A lowering storm increas'd the gloom of even,
   By warring winds the embattled clouds were driven,
And near our path a tall majestic oak,
   By the red thunderbolt in twain was riven,—
" Let us not fear," 'twas thus she mildly spoke,
" Though lightnings flash around,—our God directs
      the stroke."

How pure and rapturous are the joys that flow,
   From mutual interchange of thought and feeling,
When smile meets smile, and youthful bosom's glow,
   And eyes speak volumes, past the tongue's revealing:
   How do I love when evening's shades are stealing
Upon the landscape, and with mantle gray
   The sterner features of the scene concealing,—
With thee, Serena, thro' the fields to stray,
And mark the queen of night pursue her azure way.

What grace and beauty does her silvery ray
   Dispense, upon the dusky veil of night;
Behold the passing clouds—how dark were they!
   But now their changeful forms—how fair and bright;
   Such is the influence of thy cheering light,
Oh! love, when mutual, guileless, and serene,
   It silvers o'er each vision of delight,
And even the clouds of pensiveness are seen
'T' assume a graceful form, and wear a pleasing mien.

As with Serena once at close of day,
  I sat and watched the slowly fading scene,—
The western clouds, magnificently gay,
  Of every hue and every shape were seen,
  Like rocks or mountain heights, with vales between,
Or lofty towers, or beacons blazing high,—
  Until at length a little star serene
Shone thro' an opening that reveal'd the sky,
And there Serena turn'd and fix'd her thoughtful eye.

" Behold," said she, " that star whose placid ray
  So sweetly shines from forth the·clouded west:
'Tis thus, methinks, in life's last closing day,
  The star of Truth shall shine upon the blest,
  Tho' clouds may seem upon his path to rest;
The sun of glory on those clouds shall shine,
  And this small star, still more and more confess'd,
Shall brighter glow as earthly scenes decline,
And point the opening way, and lend her light divine."

STANZAS.

Oʜ! what are all the cares of life
  That man's devotion claim,—
Wealth's glittering toys, ambition's strife,
  And glory's splendent flame?
      'Tis not in these,
      The abode of peace
    By nature's law is given,—
      An humbler scene
      Has ever been
    The favour'd path to heaven.

'The modest primrose shuns the sight,
  In day's refulgent blaze,
But in calm evening's milder light,
  Her fragrant bloom displays;
      Thus virtue's flower,
      By wealth and power,
    From man's abode is driven,—
      While yet it blooms
      And still perfumes
    The humbler path to heaven.

Oh! give me some sequester'd spot,
  Where bounteous nature reigns,
With one—the partner of my lot—
  To share my joys and pains:
      Affection's blaze,
      Like those bright rays
    Which gild the clouds of even,
      Would loveliest shine
      In life's decline,
  And fix the eye on heaven.

EVENING ENJOYMENTS.

Come gentle eve, I long to prove
   The sweets of thy delightful reign,
When Luna walks in light above,
   And Vesper leads her starry train.

But 'tis not Luna's silvery ray,
   Nor Vesper's light I long to see,
For love, Serena, lights my way,
   And guides my gladsome steps to thee.

I haste thy tender smile to meet,
   To gaze on thy soul-beaming eye,—
To hear thy voice so soft and sweet,
   And breathe for thee affection's sigh.

Or when the pleasing cares of home
   Thy hands engage in cheerful toil,
Bright fancy's page, or wisdom's tome,
   I'll ope and read for thee, the while.

Thus, joyfully, we'll pass the eve,
   While northern tempests sweep the air,
And thus the hand of love shall weave,
   For Winter's brow, a garland fair.

And may that Power who reigns above,
   And smiles on hearts united here,
Preserve the beauteous wreath of love,
   And make it brighter every year.

STANZAS.

TO E. J.

THOUGH Nature wear a veil of gloom,
  And wintry tempests rage around,—
And through the fields bereft of bloom,
  Nor song, nor voice of joy be found;
With cheerful glance can I survey,
  The faded bower, the leafless tree,—
And with a heart o'erflowing say,
  . One blissful spot still blooms for me.

That spot serene of pure delight,
  Is thy young heart my lovely fair,
For Truth's warm sunshine clear and bright,
  On many a flower is shining there;
'Tis there the beauteous flow'rets blow,
  Of love, and faith, and constancy,
And oh! how blest am I to know
  That blissful garden blooms for me.

Oh! may no chilling frost e'er come,
　　Those flowers of Eden to destroy,
But may it still continual bloom,
　　My treasure, and my chiefest joy:
Then will I hold my peaceful way,
　　Whate'er the storms of life may be,—
And with a heart e'erflowing say,
　　One blissful spot still blooms for me.

CONNUBIAL LOVE.

ABSENT from thee, Serena, though I roam
    Through scenes sublime, that strike the ravish'd eye,
My thoughts still wander back to that dear home,
    Where thou hast cheer'd my heart in times gone by.

And when from festive halls my ear hath been
    Saluted oft with music's mirthful strain,
I still recurred to that delightful scene,
    Where peace and quiet mark thy gentle reign.

Even now, methinks, the sunny smiles I see
    Of those dear prattlers, that around thee play,
And hear the joyous shouts of mirth and glee,
    That spring from hearts as innocent as gay.

Tho' small in reason's view may be the toy,
    These youthful hearts can animate and please,—
Yet oh! how few in after life enjoy,
    Emotions undefiled and calm as these.

The joys of early life must fade away,
    Like the sweet blossoms that adorn the spring,—
Yet to the wise in their autumnal day,
    Shall heavenly truth a glorious harvest bring.

For if obedient to His high behest,
    Who calls to labour in his harvest here,
The faithful servant, even now, is blest,
    And lays up treasures for a higher sphere.

Oh! may we then each passing hour employ,
    Our little flock to lead in virtue's ways;
And may the various blessings we enjoy,
    Inspire our hearts with gratitude and praise.

Connubial love! how pleasing are the ties,
    Thou wind'st around those hearts beneath thy sway,
When all their tastes and feelings harmonise,
    And heavenly truth illuminates their way.

COSMELIA.

BEHOLD the rosy mantling glow
   On that fair cheek impress'd,
And mark the throb of silent woe,
   That heaves her tender breast.

She reads the heart-felt melting strains
   Of one no more on earth;
And while she reads, her mind regains
   The image of his worth.

She now beholds in fancy's thought
   His spirit blest above,
And hears that voice with feeling fraught
   That gain'd her virgin love.

Young William and Cosmelia were
   By tenderest feelings bound,—
More faithful he, and she more fair,
   Than all their comrades round.

But short on earth is pleasure's bloom,
    In youth's bright opening morn;
For William fills an early tomb,
    And she is left to mourn.

'T were vain indeed in fancy's dress,
    Her feelings to portray,—
One tear alone will more express,
    Than language can convey.

Yet when some token meets her eye,
    That opes the source of grief,
Her bosom heaves the secret sigh,
    Till tears afford relief.

Full many a scene of youth now seems
    To pass before her eyes,
And tender thoughts, and pleasing dreams,
    In quick succession rise.

But reason soon, too soon, alas!
    The transient bliss destroys,
And bids the pleasing vision pass
    Of all her former joys.

Oh! lovely mourner cease to grieve
    For thy departed love,
For soon together ye shall live
    In scenes of bliss above.

That gracious Power who reigns on high,
  Hath shown his guardian care,
And call'd thy William to the sky,
  That thou mayst seek him there.
    1822.

THE RE-UNION OF FRIENDS.

THERE's not a moment half so sweet,
    So fraught with heart-felt union,
As that when friends long sever'd meet,
    And join in blest communion.

Let others boast the sparkling bowl,
    Or music's softest breathing,
Or ardent strive for glory's goal,
    Their brows with laurels wreathing.

Those eyes with rapture sparkling bright,
    Can more impart of pleasure,—
Those soothing accents more delight,
    Than music's softest measure.

Why should I strive for glory's prize,
    Each care of life increasing,—
Or seek in wealth and fame to rise,
    And toil thro' life unceasing.

The bards have said, and well might say,
  This world's not worth the winning,—
Its joys continual fade away,
  Its toils are still beginning.

But ah! there is a blest retreat,
  To soothe each wounded feeling,
Where hearts expand in converse sweet,
  Their inmost thoughts revealing.

When pale disease, with reckless sway,
  Each flower of joy is stealing;
And sorrow, like a wintry day,
  Affection's buds congealing.

Then love and friendship rising bright,
  Display each scene fresh blooming,
Like spring's bright smile, with joyous light
  Fair nature's face illuming.

Should disappointment's angry frown
  Of other gifts bereave me,
Should fortune's sun in clouds go down,
  And heartless friends all leave me:

If then some kindred soul remain,
  Each gloomy moment cheering,
The seeming loss I'll count but gain,
  Our hearts the more endearing.

True love is like the diamond's glow,
In darkest hours still shining,—
To cheer the heart and soothe its woe,
When fortune's sun's declining.

FRIENDSHIP.*

ADDRESSED TO J. J. JR.

Oh! give me a friend, whose heart fraught with feeling,
Is worthy each thought of my bosom to know,
Who when each emotion my tongue is revealing,
Can share in my bliss, or can feel for my woe.

Who, when I do wrong, will feelingly chide me,
And point out the beauties of virtue and truth;
And when I am weak will never deride me,
But view with compassion the failings of youth.

Such friends there are few, in kindness they're given,
The good and the wise thro' life's voyage to cheer,
And when by adversity's gales they are driven,
The ties that unite them become still more dear.

* This is a juvenile production.

As the vine of the forest endearingly twines
Round the sov'reign of trees, the wide branching oak,
The longer it grows the more closely it binds,
Till fell'd by the axeman's dissevering stroke.

'Tis thus round the hearts of the good and the tender,
Entwine the dear feelings of friendship and love,
And when to the rude stroke of death they surrender,
Transplanted from earth, they shall flourish above.

A BIRTH-DAY ODE.

Excuse, dear girl, my serious lays,
   On such a theme, so fraught with joy,—
I know that sweet mellifluous praise
   The nicest taste will soonest cloy;
   Be mine the province then t' employ
The minstrel's art t' instruct the mind
   In joys, which naught can e'er destroy;
By time, by matter, unconfin'd,—
With age increasing still—for other worlds design'd.

A form that's beauteous to behold,—
   A soul serene that sparkles there,
Is like a diamond set in gold,
   Which monarchs might be proud to wear:
   But ah! the diamond's brilliant glare
Shines but awhile to cease with time,—
   While the pure spirit, bright and fair,
Shall soar to yet a higher clime,—
Forever rising still—to regions more sublime.

And what is life while here below?
   The best, the wisest, let them say,—
Is it a meteor's transient glow,
   To blaze a moment, then decay?
   No: 'tis the morning of a day,
Which death's dark clouds awhile obscure;
   But when those clouds shall burst away,
'Twill shine in brilliancy mature,
A bright and glorious day, that shall for aye endure.

It is the seed-time of a year,
   Whose harvest is Eternity,—
Such as we plant sojourning here,
   Such must the fruits forever be.
   How rich, how greatly blest, is he,
Who wisely shall on earth endeavour
   To plant that germ of piety,
Whose buds, nor winds nor frosts can sever,
But blooms and bears on high, forever and forever.

ELEGY

ON THE DEATH OF SAMUEL P. ADAMS.

AWAKE, my harp! thy softest strains resume,—
   'Tis friendship's voice demands thy soothing aid;
For opening genius nipt in early bloom,—
   Lamented Adams with the dead is laid,
               Low in the tomb.

Oh! youthful minstrel, tender was the tie
   That bound our hearts in unison with thine;
We mourn to think that 'neath the sod does lie
   Thy mortal part,—but ah! the spark divine
               Shall never die.

But death to thee wore no appalling mien,—
   Familiar to thy thoughts was his dread blow,
And often thou at evening's hour serene,
   In some lone spot, " with solemn steps and slow,"
               Wast musing seen.

'Then did thy harp attune that solemn lay,
   Which seem'd to presage thy departing hour,
Then did thy soul resign'd, in wisdom say,
   To life's delusive splendours, wealth and power,
             Vain shades, away!

Oh! how the soul, at solemn times like this,
   Leaves far below her anxious cares and pains,—
On wings of faith flies o'er the dread abyss,
   Until she reaches that bright realm, where reigns
             Eternal bliss.

And how this fleeting world's unreal show
   Fades from the view at this calm thoughtful hour,—
'Tis at such times the soul is taught to know,
   " Virtue's the only amaranthine flower"
             That blooms below.

But ah! not long the youthful bard was doom'd
   T' indulge bright fancy's rapture beaming ray,—
For ьoon disease his rising morn o'ergloom'd,
   And now from these lov'd haunts—far, far away
             He lies entomb'd

Oh! pale consumption, reckless is thy sway,
   Thou faithful messenger of God's decree;
Changeful and slow thy victim's sure decay,
   Like some dim taper's fitful blaze we see
             Flickering away.

   11*

But why should man so dread thy leveling hand,
  In mercy sent life's pleasures to destroy;
Yes, sent by Heavenly Love's benign command,
  To fit the soul by trials here, t' enjoy
            A happier land.

Oh! who to leave this spot we love so well,
  Without some previous warning, would desire?
Who would not wish some kindred soul to tell
  His last request, or say, ere life expire,
            A long farewell?

Whene'er this frail existence I resign,
  May I not sink with unexpected blow,—
But, if the will of Providence divine,
  May some disease, life's pulse destroying slow,
            My soul refine.

For what are all the pains we feel on earth,
  Compar'd with that inestimable prize,
That " pearl of price," more than all treasures worth,
  Which gives a title to serener skies,
            A heavenly birth.

But let us not await till death draws nigh;
  For soon and unexpected it may come;
Far wiser 'twere in early life to try,
  By righteousness, to gain a lasting home
            With God on high.

That stroke, which both the coward and the brave
   Alike awaits,—for both alike must die,—
That stroke, from which no earthly power can save,
   We too must feel,—like Adams we must lie
            Low in the grave,

LINES

ADDRESSED TO A FRIEND, ON THE DEATH OF HIS
FATHER.

'Tis not the love of praise inspires this lay,
  With glittering thoughts to gild the elegiac line ;
'Tis friendship's voice,—and only means to say,
  My bosom feels a kindred throb with thine.
    When forms belov'd, in death's embrace recline,
And the free spirit leaves this dark sojourn,
  To seek the bosom of its Sire divine ;
Oh ! let us not a change so blissful, mourn,
Nor pine at Heaven's decree, nor wish the soul's return.

But for ourselves, some sorrowing tears must fall,
  Some fervent sighs will heave the troubled breast,
And while we bow before the imperious call,
  That takes his spirit to the realms of rest,
    Oh ! let us praise the Almighty's kind behest,
Which lent us for a pure example here,
  A kindred soul with such perfections blest,
And now hath call'd him from his bright career,
With age and honour crown'd, to fill a higher sphere.

His faithful consort mourns her hapless doom,
　　His youthful children heave the heart-felt sigh,—
Teach these, my friend, to look beyond the tomb,
　　Where not a tear shall dim the christian's eye:
　　Methinks I hear his voice paternal cry,
" My children, follow in the path I've trod"—
　　Methinks I see him, beckoning from on high,
To call the wanderers from this dark abode,
To realms of bliss above—the bosom of our God.

But still, my friend, one tender charge thou hast,
　　That most of all requires thy sympathy,—
One tender plant that shrinks before the blast,
　　And needs that shelter which she finds in thee :
　　Continue still, a brother thus to be;
Forget thine own, a sister's grief to share,
　　Wipe from her eyes the tears of piety,—
And while thy recompense thou readest there,
Still with a brother's love, combine a father's care

AFFLICTION.

Though long upon the willow tree has hung
My harp,—or only in the lonely hours
Of solitude, been swept by sorrow's hand,—
Fain would I bring, dear sister, to thine ear,
Some soothing lay to cheer th' afflictive hour.
And shall I sing the joy affliction brings?
How it becomes the messenger of Heaven,
To call us from our earthly loves and cares,
And fix our thoughts on purer things above?
Oh! I have felt how gently it unclasps,
The tendrils that we twine around those weeds
Of earth,—which were too weak for our support;
And how it gives a surer, stronger stay,
To lift dependent man above the dust,
In the bright sunshine of eternal love;
And when the tempest rages, to uphold
The trembling soul.   Thou too hast felt these things;
Thou hast, I trust, found Him, of whom 'tis said
That " Moses and the prophets spake,"—himself

While here on earth, a life of sorrow led;
And is it strange that they whom he designs
To reign with him, should share his sufferings too.
" He chasteneth whom he loveth,"—let us then,
Dear sister, raise to Him the incense pure,
Of gratitude for all his favours past;
Even for afflictions,—which, like clouds and rain,
Obscure awhile the brightness of our sky,—
But are the means appointed to bring forth
The tender plant, and to sustain its life.
Yet are there times, even in the darkest days,
When light shines thro' the broken clouds, and brings
Before the mental eye, that heavenly bow,
Which gives the promise of a purer sky,
Where Truth celestial shall unclouded shine,
And love and mercy reign forever more.

CALORIC.

COMPANION of the sunbeam !—thy swift flight,
Though felt by all, eludes all human sight:
Throughout the realms of earth, and air, and sea,
What various forms of matter, spring from thee.
   Thou wast the agent of Eternal might,
That rear'd the Andes to their lofty height;
By thee driv'n forth the imprison'd vapours fled,
Retiring ocean show'd his rocky bed,
And earth was shaken with convulsive throes,
When from the yawning gulf, the mountains rose.
   On Ætna's peak where burning embers glow,
Or streams of lava from Vesuvius flow,—
Thine is the power, that in the abyss profound,
Subdues the molten mass that boils around,
Sends up the flaming flood in columns bright,
And sheds o'er sea and land, a beacon light.
   To milder scenes now turn the excursive eye,
And watch the mists that o'er yon landscape lie,—
In fleecy whiteness on the lake they sleep,
Or spread their curtains o'er the valleys deep;

But as the rising sun with splendour glows,
What varied beauties do their forms disclose,—
Till on the morning's wings they rise on high,
And sail majestic, thro' the azure sky.
Whence is the power that thus can elevate
The sluggish waters from their liquid state,
And in the regions of the upper air,
The boundless magazine of storms prepare?—
Thine is that mighty force, Caloric, thine,
Thou unseen minister of power Divine.

When joyous Spring advances o'er the land,
And flowers put forth, and budding leaves expand,—
'Tis genial heat that gives the violet birth,
And with luxuriant verdure clothes the earth ;
And when bright Summer pours his radiance down,
The fruits to ripen, and the harvests crown ;
And sober Autumn follows in his train,
Replete with luscious grapes and golden grain :
Throughout each season, every change we see,
Agent of power Divine ! is wrought by thee.
From thee, when Winter's blast is howling round,
Comfort and joy within our homes are found,—
'Tis then the social circle, gather'd there,
Resigns each toil, forgets each anxious care ;
And while the blazing pile consumes away,
In social converse flies the wintry day.

From these clear proofs of wisdom and design,
To thee we turn, great Architect Divine.

Ere yon resplendent sun his course began,
Thine eye omniscient trac'd the glorious plan,—
To each revolving sphere its place assign'd,
And in one perfect system, all combin'd:
Nor less conspicuous shines thy guardian care,
In every fragrant flower that scents the air,
In every insect form that meets the eye,
Than in yon radiant orbs that roll on high.

If in these lower works such charms we find,
How far transcendent is the world of mind:
The fairest forms on earth must soon decay,
Yon radiant orbs themselves may pass away;
But seeds of virtue sown in weakness here,
Shall bloom and flourish in a higher sphere,—
Devotion's flame more brightly shall ascend,
And the full-tide of joy shall never end.

LIGHT.

" HAIL holy Light! offspring of Heaven first born,"*
Ere yet the earth was form'd,—while darkness lay
Like a broad mantle o'er the vast abyss,
The Great Supreme, sole source of light and life,
His vital spirit breath'd upon the deep,
And call'd from nothing thy refulgent beams;
Myriads of suns at his command shot forth,
And took their stations in the void immense.
'Twas then our earth with her attendant moon,
And all the planets with their satellites,
Began their journey thro' the fields of space,
And join'd the anthem from unnumber'd worlds,
When all the sons of God shouted for joy.
Bright orb of day! how numerous are the forms
That on thy beams depend! when first thy rays
Dawn in the east with mild refracted light,
What graceful shapes the attendant clouds assume,
As in their gorgeous liveries array'd,—

They crowd around thy throne.   The morning dews,
Like glittering diamonds hung from every spray,
Drink thy pure beams, till more ethereal grown,
They rise to meet thee in the fields of air.
The opening flowers their fragrant incense shed,
Their budding leaves expand,—and every plant
With brightening verdure owns thy genial sway.
  But most of all, by animated life
Thy quickening power is felt.   The feather'd tribes
Attune their notes, and fill the groves with song.
The soaring lark springs up at thy approach,
And from mid-air his joyful strain sends forth,
While flocks and herds the general anthem join.
  But half the wonders by thy light produc'd,
From man's research lay hid, till Newton came,
And with the aid of his prismatic glass,
Thy beams refracted, and disclos'd to view
The rainbow's colours in a ray of light:
He show'd to wondering man that all the tints
With which fair Nature paints her loveliest scenes,
From thy pure beams are drawn.   The dazzling red.
The orange, and the yellow's paler hues,
The lively green in which the fields are clad,
The pure deep azure that adorns the sky,
The indigo and violet; and all
The nicely blended shades from these combin'd.
  How simple, yet how grand, the works of God!
Sent forth by him, the particles of light

Traverse with joy the boundless fields of space,
Nor change their course till at the earth arriv'd,
They yield obedience to refraction's law,
Bend from their course to cheer the eye of man,
To clothe the earth with verdure, and to give
To every living thing the means of life.
Fit emblem they, of that Eternal Power,
Who form'd mankind,—and loves what he has form'd :
Alike upon the evil and the good
He makes his sun to rise, his rains descend ;
But most of all the dedicated heart
His goodness shares,—'tis there he sheds a ray
More pure than that which lights the outward world,—
A ray of light Divine,—which as it dawns
Upon the mind, and gains dominion there,
Opens a fountain of unmingled bliss.
'Tis then the affections and desires become
Plants of the Father's love, water'd by dews
From heaven, bearing fruits for heaven design'd,
And yielding even here, in peace and joy,
A lively foretaste of the eternal world.

ELECTRICITY.

MYSTERIOUS agent of the Great Supreme !
　How bright thy course, how rapid is thy flight,
When o'er the heavens the vivid lightnings gleam,
　And streams of glory crown the polar night.

How would the rigors of the Arctic clime,
　The germs of Fancy and of Hope destroy,—
Did not thy radiant cross, and arch sublime,
　Shoot o'er the heavens and fill the earth with joy.

The fur-clad Indian from his cave of snow,
　Comes forth rejoicing at the glorious sight,
Beholds the heavens above with splendour glow,
　And tow'ring glaciers sparkling in the light.

Though uninstructed in that sacred lore,
　Which tells the wonders of redeeming love ;
A secret influence bids his heart adore
　That Power unseen, whose glory shines above.

Nor less the greatness of that Power is seen,
   When o'er the regions of the torrid zone,
Comes forth the monsoon,—and the lightning's sheen,
   Thro' clouds and tempests flashes round his throne.

How dread the thunder's peal that rolls above !
   How bright the flashes that illume the sky !
Yet even in these are seen the unbounded love
   Of Him whose power and wisdom rule on high :

His ministers are these, to purify
   The noxious vapours in those regions found,—
To fill the mountain springs, the lakes supply,
   And the full-tide of plenty pour around.

But see ! the storm is past, yon eastern cloud
   Reflects the rainbow from its dripping shower,—
Forth from their tents the joyous natives crowd,
   To inhale the freshness of the evening hour.

What tho' fair Science to their mental eye,
   Creation's hidden charms hath not reveal'd,—
They see the beauty of the azure sky,
   And gaze with rapture on the verdant field.

In that bright region of perennial flowers,
   What rich enjoyment would these scenes impart,
Did science and devotion's blended powers
   Illume the mind and purify the heart.

For 'tis the heart that needs the genial ray
  Of light Divine its darkness to assuage,
And cheer the pilgrim on his dreary way,
    When clouds hang o'er him, and when tempests rage.

And when at length those clouds shall break away,
    As the still evening hour of life draws nigh,—
'Tis heavenly Truth illumes the closing day,
    And Hope's bright rainbow cheers the christian's
      eye.

ASTRONOMY.

How do I love when Evening spreads her veil,
And Silence keeps her secret watch around,
To cast aside the anxious cares of life,
And hold communion with the starry spheres.
   Still, as the glimmering day-light fades away,
The constellations one by one emerge ;
Scarce seen at first amid the depths of ether,
But soon more numerous, more refulgent glow,
Till all the sky is spangled with their blaze.
   But see ! with graceful step fair Science comes !
Her optic tube she holds before our sight,
And countless stars, lost to unaided vision,
Burst forth from darkness on the raptur'd view :
In every star another sun we trace,
Round which vast worlds unceasingly revolve,
And likewise these encircled by their moons,
Harmonious, moving in their lesser spheres.
But still the mind would soar beyond this scene,
And thoughtful muse on Him—the Great Supreme,

Who, like a shepherd on some eminence,
'That watches o'er his flock, beholds with joy
Their sportive gambols o'er the extended plain.
   How sinks vain boastful man in nothingness
With such a scene compar'd !   What is our earth,
This little scene of tumult and turmoil,
Where warriors strive for empire,—statesmen grasp
The phantom power,—and misers gather dust !
   Oh ! say, ye radiant orbs that wheel thro' space,
In distance vast, in number infinite,—
Lives there upon your surfaces a race,
Like ours in form, like ours of transcient date,
And fallen like ours from pristine purity ?
   To say ye shine for us, and us alone,
Presumption's height would be,—shall those vast orbs
Form'd like our earth, but how much more immense !
Wheel through the deserts of infinity,
And waft no praises to their Maker's ear ?
Reason forbids.   Methinks I see the forms
Of beings like ourselves move thro' the scene :
Fain would I hope, more pure, more blest than we.
Perhaps amid those worlds to us unknown,
Some blooming Edens yet there may remain,
Where man, the image of his Sire divine,
Still tastes the raptures of unsullied bliss.
Perhaps those countless myriads yet are pure,
And ours the only world defil'd with sin.
   But these are subjects hidden from our search,—

In bounteous wisdom hid,—for could we see
The just amount of our own littleness,
And magnitude immense of Power divine,
Hope would expire amid the blaze of Truth.
Oh! how immense His goodness then who breathes
His quickening spirit thro' the universe,—
Controls the movements of the vast machine,
And all its light and energy imparts :
Who not alone permits our being here,
But makes his dwelling with the pure in heart.

Should we not then to nobler life aspire,
Cast off the cares which bind us down to earth,
And hail the approach of that auspicious day,
When the dark veil which now obscures our sight,
By death shall be withdrawn,—and the pure soul
Soar thro' the regions of infinity,
All light, and life, intelligence and joy.

ATTRACTION.

THROUGHOUT material things the power is known
    Of one attractive law which binds the whole,—
In smallest atoms is its presence shown,
    And suns and planets prove its vast control.

The flaming comet, this restraining force
    Calls from his wanderings thro' the fields of space;
Around the sun he takes his fiery course,
    Then starts impetuous on his distant race.

Impell'd by this, each satellite attends
    Her guardian planet, and his journey cheers,—
And on this power unseen, the sun depends
    To guide the movements of his circling spheres.

And does there not exist a power like this,
    The human soul to regulate and bind?
The wisdom of the past proclaims there is
    A law as potent in the world of mind.

It is the power of truth and love divine,
   A law to regulate, a light to cheer,—
Within the path of duty to confine,
   Or call the wanderer from his wild career.

But on material things, the force impress'd
   In their primeval hour, preserves them still,—
While man alone, with conscious freedom blest,
   Has left the orbit he was form'd to fill.

Yet aspirations pure, and thoughts sublime,
   By heavenly love are breath'd upon the soul,
Design'd to call us from the things of time,
   And guide our spirits to their destin'd goal.

13

THE TRIUMPHS OF TRUTH.

This is the *first part* of a Poem intended to illustrate the christian doctrine of non-resistance, and to show that the gospel has always been advanced by the sufferings of the faithful.

WHAT was it gave to Eden all its bloom,
And all its brightness to the morn of time?
Was it that Nature wore a fairer form,—
The gentler swell of undulating hills,—
The bloom of forests, or the beauteous robe
Of vallies, clad in never-failing flowers?
Was it the lapse of sweetly murmuring rills,
Or rivers flowing musically soft,
O'er golden sands and many sparkling gems?
Was it the voice of Nature's tuneful choir,
Melodious warbling from the green retreats,
Or angels' harps from neighbouring summits heard?
Oh! no, methinks it was the beauteous robe
Of innocence, that cloth'd the human soul;
'Twas in the heart of man the precious streams
Of consolation flowed. 'Twas from the mind,

The heaven-born mind, that angel music rose:
For all the affections and desires of man,
Like angels, then administer'd to joy.
How shall we now "the blissful seat regain?"
'Tis by obedience to that Living Word
In every heart reveal'd,—which separates
The precious from the vile, and only slays
Those lusts impure that war against the soul.
Then opens to new life the heaven-born mind,
And feels a relish for sublimer joy.

How sinks all worldly glory in his view,
Whose eyes are open'd to behold the charms
Of heavenly truth! he sees on every hand
The obvious traces of a Power divine,
And in his bosom feels the kindling glow
Of that celestial love which wide extends,
Embracing all the family of man.

What is the gorgeous pomp of martial life,
Where victory rides triumphant o'er the slain,
And holds the laurel o'er the hero's brow?
While meagre want, and pain, and dire disease,
Are prowling round the field, intent to grasp
The wretch forlorn, and bear him to his doom?
Oh! what are these, Celestial Love! compar'd
With thy angelic charms, and blissful train
Of virtues pure, and graces from on high.
And yet, how blind are men! the husbandman
Whose arduous labour clears the forest wild,

With waving harvests, crowns the breezy hill,
The verdant carpet spreads along the vale,
The granary rears where rich abundance reigns,
And mansion fair, where sons and daughters dwell:
When he departs, scarce are his virtues known
Beyond the precincts of his native vale.
  But see! a warrior comes,—the mansion fires,—
The granary plunders,—slays the lowing herd,
And scatters devastation o'er the fields:
But oh! sweet counterpart of all this woe,
He saves a shrieking fair-one from the flames
Himself hath kindled,—then is blazon'd forth
The hero's name, so generous and so brave.
The bard, enraptur'd with the warlike theme,
In glowing verse portrays his mighty deeds,
With the soft music of his numbers drowns
The soldier's dying shriek, the widow's moan,
The orphan's plaintive cry; and even persuades
Destroying Time to spare a name so dear.
Thus youthful hearts are taught to venerate
The hero's name, for martial glory pant—
Spurn the kind offers of redeeming love,
And rush impetuous to the field of strife.
But oh! Celestial Love, be thou my theme,
Whose reign was promis'd by the heavenly choir,
When erst the babe of Bethlehem was born.
In him thy spirit dwelt in fulness then,
And with thy people still in measure dwells,

Proclaiming peace on earth, good-will to men.
Tho' meek and lowly does thy form appear
To him whose eye is dazzled by the blaze
Of martial fame, yet do they hold thee dear,
Whose hearts are touch'd with thy celestial flame,
Whose eyes are open'd to behold the joys
That from obedience to thy dictates flow.
How hast thou suffer'd in the sons of men,
And how the sufferings of the righteous seed
In every age, have been the means ordain'd,
The light of truth to spread, the hearts of men
To subjugate,—and even to draw forth
From persecuting zeal, a pitying tear.
Behold the sufferings of the Son of God,
And mark the triumph by those sufferings wrought!
He came to bear a testimony pure
To heavenly Truth:—to manifest on earth
The love unspeakable of God to man.
At every step his progress was oppos'd
By bigotry, hypocrisy, and pride.
Their errors he condemn'd, their pride reprov'd,
And all their vile hypocrisy expos'd.
They rose against him, and he meekly bore
Their taunts and their derision,—when they smote,
His unresisting form was like the sheep
Before its shearers, dumb: the stripes severe,
By their iniquity impos'd,—the crown
And purple robe, in mockery put on,
    13*

And even the tortures of that lingering death
Caus'd not a murmur to escape his lips.
At that dread hour, the heavens were veil'd in gloom,
And earth affrighted, with convulsions shook;
Yet still the patient sufferer on the cross,
Look'd down benignly on the sons of men.

    He saw in distant vision all the woes
Jerusalem must suffer, when her sons
In deadly strife should drench her streets in blood;
While at her gates, and round her tottering walls
Her enemies are gather'd.   Then his heart
Was touch'd with pity for rebellious man,
And for his murderers arose that prayer,
"Father forgive, they know not what they do."
Not all the signs and miracles perform'd,
Nor yet the powerful preaching of the word,
Nor even th' example of his spotless life,
Had touch'd the hearts of that obdurate race.
But now their hearts misgave them; he was gone,
On whose mild brow had goodness sat enthron'd,
From whose pure lips those heavenly accents flow'd,
On which the multitude enraptur'd hung,
And felt the impulse of a power divine.

    Now they remember'd how his life had past
In works of love and peace,—how he had cheer'd
The widow, and restor'd her son to life;
How he had cleans'd the leper, whose hard lot
Was from all human sympathy cut off;

And how benign he look'd, when in his arms
He took their little children, and proclaim'd
Of such as these my kingdom shall be form'd.

  Behold, the time of Pentecost is come,
From all the earth are pilgrims gather'd now,
To celebrate with pomp the solemn rites
Of that eventful day: but where is he
By whom that multitude has oft been taught,
That prophet whom they hop'd would yet restore
The kingdom unto Israel.   He is slain,
And in the sepulchre his body laid;
Yet is it whisper'd thro' the anxious crowd,
That he still lives and has been seen of men.

  Now come the Apostles forth, and Peter first
Proclaims the joyful news that Christ is risen.
" The prophecies of old are thus fulfill'd—
The stone which ye rejected has become
Head of the corner: and the Prince of life,
Is he, whose blood your guilty hands have shed."
How are they conscience-stricken! every word
Is by the witness in their hearts confirm'd,
And the vast multitude is bow'd and shaken,
As when a mighty wind sweeps thro' the ranks
Of forest trees, and bends their lofty pride.

  And now they cry, with one accord, to him
Whom they have oft rejected; and he hears
In boundless love their penitential prayer,
And through his spirit's purifying power,

Saves by baptising in the stream of life.
Behold the riches of redeeming love:
Those stony hearts which nothing else could move,
Which all the power of his persuasive word,
And all the force of miracles withstood,
Were touch'd and melted by the dying love
And patient sufferings of the Son of God.

A fire was kindled then,—destin'd to spread
Throughout the earth,—and by its power subdue
And bring to naught, the idols of mankind.
But ah! the votaries of that sacred flame,
Who felt its influence burning in their hearts,
And there subjecting all things to itself;
How were they doomed to suffer!   Yet they knew
When the good Shepherd call'd them to his fold,
That as he trod thro' life, a thorny path,
And suffer'd to reclaim his wandering sheep,
So must they follow in his steps, and be
Partakers of his sufferings and his joys.

First of the martyrs, righteous Stephen died,
Or rather, pass'd triumphant into life,
Whilst in a glorious vision, he beheld
The Son of man in heavenly bliss enthron'd.

But who is he amidst the angry crowd,
That urges forward their relentless hate,
And stands a witness of the martyr's death?
'Tis persecuting Saul.   Strict in the law,
Of morals most exact,—a Pharisee,

Bred at Gamaliel's feet,—his mind is stor'd
With theologian lore,—but ah! his heart
Fill'd with intolerance and bigotry,
Has never known the work of saving grace.
Yet even to him does Love Divine extend,
And as he journeys forward, fill'd with rage,
And breathing threats against the flock of Christ,
Soon is his course arrested: he beholds
A glorious light from heaven around him shine,
A voice of stern reproof salutes his ear,
And in that vision is he shewn the Lamb
Whom he has persecuted. See him now,
How changed! how humbled! ready to forgive,
And suffer all things for the sake of Christ.
Most valiant in the cause he has espous'd,
He journeys forth to many a distant land,
The herald of the cross,—the champion bold,
Whom tortures cannot move, nor death appal.
  Oh! Love Divine, how does thy power subdue
The fiercest passions of the human heart,
And cause the lion and the lamb to dwell
In peace, where thou dost reign. The free-born soul
Is not compelled to serve,—for liberty
Is an essential attribute of mind,
Which God will not destroy. He placed us here
Our faithfulness to prove, and gave us power
To choose or to reject his proffer'd grace.
Desires and appetites has he conferr'd,

Which though essential to our being, here,
And all conducive to our highest bliss
When under his control,—yet when, depriv'd
Of his directing power, they take the throne
And rule in our affections, how they bring
The soul in bondage and degrade its powers:
Then are the beasts of prey let loose; and man
Goes forth the enemy of man,—destroys
That life which God alone can give,
And while himself the slave of lust and pride,
Becomes the oppressor of his fellow man.

Oh! may thy kingdom come, great Prince of Peace,
And first of all, may they who bear thy name,
Know thy meek spirit in their hearts prevail;
Then shall thy doctrines like the dew distil,
And distant nations own thy blissful reign.

'Twas thus that Paul went forth, dependent now
Not on the broken reed of classic lore,
Or speculative science:—prostrate lay
The structure proud of his ambitious youth,
He counted all but dross, so he might win
That wisdom pure, descended from above,
Which is dispensed to babes:—and when he spake,
'Twas not with eloquence of man's device,
But even with fear and trembling,—and the fire
Of holy love that kindled in his heart
And strove for utterance, burst forth a flame
That swept all things before it: all the art

And sophistry of priests could not withstand
The inward evidence and melting power,
Of that Eternal Word by which he spake.
  Oh! what a band of valiants then went forth,
To spread the gospel banner, and to give
To nations long benighted, light and truth:
Successors of the Apostles; Prophets call'd
Of the New Testament,—undaunted men
In whom the Spirit of Truth was manifest,
Tho' uninstructed in scholastic lore,
And labouring for their bread; yet were they taught
In wisdom more sublime, than all the schools
Of Egypt or of Athens could impart.
  Nor were ye left behind in works of love,
Mothers and sisters of the martyr band!
The last to leave the spot where Jesus died,
The first to witness his triumphant rise,
And bear his message to the sons of men.
How steadfast was your faith! how pure your love!
When call'd to suffer for his glorious cause,
Or when, with wisdom from on high endued,
Sent forth the ministers of God to man.
  How did thy light break forth and spread,
O Zion! city of the living God!
The nations flocked to thee, from the far north
Where Scandinavian forests spread their gloom,
Even to the south, where Ethiopia's sons
Imploring help, stretch'd forth their hands to God.

But now the time draws nigh, when all your faith,
Your constancy and love, will be requir'd:
Behold! the beast of Pagan Rome is rous'd,
By rage impelled, by superstition led,
Constraining all, his impious rites to join.
 The blood of saints and martyrs flows profuse:
Pursued with fire and sword, by tortures racked,
And in the amphitheatre expos'd
To all the fury of ferocious beasts;
A spectacle by multitudes enjoy'd,
More cruel and ferocious still than they.
Yet how triumphant did your faith appear!
E'en in the midst of torments could ye sing
The praise of Him whose all-sustaining word
Dwelt in your hearts, the living source of joy.
Then did thy kingdom spread, Emmanuel!
Won by that power which in thy servants dwelt,
His bloody sword the heathen warrior sheath'd,
And shap'd to arts of peace the glittering spear,
Renouncing all the implements of war.
Behold how fair the faithful spouse of Christ;
Her spotless garments are of "linen fine,"
"The righteousness of saints," from heaven sent down
T' adorn and dignify the human soul:
Each mild perfection and commanding grace
In her is seen united, while she goes
Upon her way rejoicing, and the light
Of heavenly Truth is shining on her path.

THE MARTYRS.

WHILE Rome, the mistress of the world, remain'd
 In base submission to the Tyrant's rod,
The meek disciples of the Lamb attain'd
 The glorious freedom of the sons of God.

What tho' in suffering they were doom'd to bear
 The Martyr's cross, e'en to their latest breath;
Yet these afflictions they rejoic'd to share,
 With him who triumphed o'er the power of death.

While in their view the glittering crown appears,
 Which waits the Martyr in the realms above,
'Twas thus, methinks, triumphant o'er their fears,
 They sang the praises of Redeeming Love:

"To thee we turn our thoughts, Eternal One!
 Who form'd the worlds by thy resistless might,
And through the glorious gospel of thy Son,
 Brought life and immortality to light.

14

" Do thou be with us in that trying hour,
  When nature yields to agonizing pain;
Even in our weakness manifest thy power,
  Through life to succour, and in death sustain.

" We ask not vengeance on the tyrant's head,
  Whose rage consigns us to the Martyr's stake,
But may thy glorious kingdom ever spread,
  And may our spirits of its joys partake.

" Thy heavenly image in our hearts renew,
  And may thy spirit in our minds appear,
Even as the ' sunbeam in a drop of dew'*
  Shines, and exalts it to a higher sphere."
        1838.

* "As shines the sunbeam in a drop of dew."
                                Russian Anthology.

LUCY'S GRAVE.*

SAY, maiden, say! why art thou here,
The midnight hour is drawing near,
   'Tis darkness all around;
The stars are twinkling from on high,
The night winds too begin to sigh,
And hark! the owlet seated nigh,
   Emits a mournful sound.

"I watch," the lovely maniac said,
"O'er Lucy's cold and lowly bed,
   Until the moon appear;
For here does she unconscious sleep,
And here at eve I come to weep
Beside her grave, and constant keep
   A nightly vigil near.

* This Ballad was written many years ago,—the incidents on
which it is founded, were taken from a work called the "New
England Tale."

"In these green bays with which I'm crown'd,
With which her grave is strew'd around,
    Her emblem we may see;
For she was lovely, young, and gay,
As beauteous and as fresh as they,
But soon by death was snatch'd away,
    From off her parent tree.

"She lov'd, oh! yes, she fondly lov'd,—
Her William too as faithful prov'd,—
    Their hearts were both sincere:
How sweetly did they walk the vale,
While o'er each heart did love prevail:
He told his artless, tender tale,
    Nor loath was she to hear.

"But civil discord soon arose,
More dreadful far than foreign foes,
    And spread confusion round;
To quell the rebels William sped,*
From Lucy's soothing voice he fled,
To hear the groaning of the dead,
    And trumpet's martial sound.

* The rebellion here alluded to, was an attempt made by Capt
Shay and others, to resist the laws of Massachusetts in the year
1786.

"But in a dark unguarded hour,
O'ertaken by superior power,
   A captive he was led;
To advance, the rebels now began,—
Among his friends the rumour ran,
They'd placed him in the battle's van,
   To strike the foe with dread.

"His comrades now advancing bold,
All stand aghast when they behold
   The captive warrior there;
But soon the hatred of their foes,
And memory of their country's woes,
O'er every tender feeling rose,
   For combat they prepare.

"'Twas then we saw young Lucy's form,
Like mercy's angel 'midst the storm,
   With fearless footsteps fly,—
For mercy's sake, she cried, forbear;
Oh! spare your faithful comrade, spare,
And on you shall my constant prayer
   Call blessings from on high.

"Her fainting form they bear away;
The fiery war-horse seeks the fray,
   And heeds the curb no more:
Now sulphurous flames each host surround,
  14*

The cannons pour the bellowing sound,
And hills and forests trembling round,
   Repeat the dreadful roar.

" Beneath his friends' own galling fire,
Did youthful William then expire—
   The ball had pierced his heart:
To Lucy's arms his corse they bore,—
She press'd his bosom, stain'd with gore,
But ah ! from her pale lips no more
   Did word or sigh depart.

" His form so firmly did she clasp,
That scarcely could they loose her grasp—
   The last long grasp of love ;
And when they laid him 'neath the sod,
Her spirit loath'd its dark abode,
And straitway flew to meet its God,
   In purer realms above.

" Oh ! civil war, thou worst of strife,
Thou greatest bane of human life,
   What woes on thee await,—
How dost thou rend the dearest ties,
Call'd up by thee, what furies rise,
Till life itself, that dearest prize,
   Becomes a loathsome state.

" But see yon eastern streaks of light,
The moon will rise and watch to night
  O'er Lucy's lowly bed,—
She loves to look and linger near
This spot, to youth and virtue dear,
And many a dewy, sparkling tear,
  Around the grave will shed."

As these last words the maniac said,
She left the dwelling of the dead,
  Nor cast one glance behind;
Methought, as thence I took my way,
There's naught so mournful to survey
As this frail tenement of clay,
  Deserted by the mind.

Let others roam to foreign climes,
Where grandeur reign'd in ancient times,
  Now strew'd with ruins o'er,
And say, " Here rolls the Tiber's flood,
'Twas here the Coliseum stood,
And here the faithful martyr's blood
  Was shed in days of yore."

'Tis more affecting far to me
This lovely maniac's form to see,
  Than works of human hands :

The latest work of heavenly care
Was woman's form divinely fair,
But see, this temple past repair,
   A desert ruin stands.

EVENING REFLECTIONS.

Oh ! how I love, at evening's close,
   When day's last lingering beams decay,
In sweet secluded calm repose,
   To sit and muse the hours away.

Not till the sun's resplendent blaze,
   The mountain's western verge has sought,
The moon her crescent pale displays,
   To soothe the soul to solemn thought.

'Tis not till present scenes around
   Have faded with the fading day,
Will memory's silvery light be found,
   To bring the soul beneath her sway.

Oh ! memory, sweet consoling power,
   On earth thy lot is kindly cast,
To cheer each solitary hour,
   With pleasures borrow'd from the past.

The scenes of early life, I see,
   And youthful friends around me stand:
So clear,—so plain,—they seem to be
   Returning from a distant land.

At such an hour I feel like those
   Who skim the ocean's waveless breast,
When evening's shades around them close,
   And mildest zephyrs soothe to rest.

Far from the busy haunts of life,
   They keep their noiseless, peaceful way,
Nor hear the world's discordant strife,
   Nor feel the passions' ruthless sway.

Although the smooth, unruffled tide,
   Still bears them onward from their homes,
In dreams, with fancy's wings supplied,
   Round that lov'd spot the seaman roams.

He hears the voice of friendship greet,
   With cheering words, his safe return,—
And sees that glance, so witching sweet,
   Which makes the heart with rapture burn.

'Tis thus amid my waking dreams,
   I fly o'er Time's swift rolling wave,
And join my friends in distant scenes,
   Or call them from the dreary grave.

'Tis at this hour that fancy's flight
    Beyond the realms of present day,
Far through futurity's dark night,
    Pursues her swift adventurous way.

'Tis then she sees those visions bright
    Of future days and happier times,
And dreams of that supreme delight
    Reserved alone for purer climes,—

Beholds a region where no storms
    Shall mar the loveliness of day,
Communes with purer, happier forms,
    Which reason's light must chase away.

But ah! the dreams she then pursues,
    Like western clouds at close of day,
Assume a thousand forms and hues,
    As fleeting, though as bright, as they.

LINES

WRITTEN IN AN ALBUM.

METHINKS an emblem of the cultur'd mind,
The rich and varied Album was design'd;
Friendship and love, like amaranthine flowers,
Bloom here, selected from unnumber'd bowers;
And taste and genius each succeeding year,
Shall bring fresh flowers to shed their fragrance here.
Fain would I plant in this delightful spot,
That little modest flower,—Forget-me-not:
And oh! how happy, could I dare presume,
'Twere worth transplanting in *thy heart* to bloom.

MENTAL BEAUTY.

'TELL not of Persia's blue ey'd maids,
   With golden locks so graceful flowing,—
'Tell not of Cashmere's flowery glades,
   With spicy-fragrant zephyrs blowing.

Though bleak the clime, and rough the land,
   Give me Columbia's free-born nation,
Where Beauty's fairest flowers expand,
   Beneath the beams of Education.

Give me the intellectual glance,
   Reason's ethereal light revealing—
The mental glow, that can entrance
   The human soul with tenderest feeling.

The lovely Persian's azure eye,
   With Nature's warm expression beaming,
May raise the floods of passion high
   With rapture, but with danger teeming.

15

But to behold this mental glow,
   The soul o'erflows with soft emotion,—
Mild as the tides, delighted, flow,
   When Luna smiles upon the ocean.

TO OPHELIA.

WRITTEN FOR AN ALBUM.

On thee, Ophelia, youth's enlivening ray
Shines brightly now, and gilds thy flowery way,—
Hope calls thee forward to her fairy bowers,
And love and friendship gladden all thy hours.
The minstrel's art is needless then, to cheer
Thy heart with music, or to soothe thine ear;
For sorrow's note that ear hath seldom met,—
The vernal sounds of youth float round it yet;
That heart, methinks, is innocent and gay,
And needs no song to chase its cares away.
For me, I trust, the nobler task remains,
To breathe instruction in the minstrel's strains,—
To warn the youthful heart that those bright flowers,
Which bloom in Pleasure's fascinating bowers,
Will droop and fall in our autumnal day,
And lose their fragrance. ere they fade away.

But let not Virtue mourn the early fate,
Of things unworthy of a longer date,—
For there are flowers that shall survive the tomb,
And shed their fragrance in immortal bloom—
Those which are planted by that Power above,
Whose ways are goodness, and whose name is Love.

FAREWELL TO THE HARP.*

Farewell, my Harp! I'm loath to say farewell!
But not for aye, I trust, thou'lt cease thy flow;
How oft the influence of thy witching spell
Hath rais'd my raptures, and hath soothed my woe.

But 'tis not meet that fancy's restless wing
Should from ourselves, our scrutiny withhold;
Mark how the fairest products of the spring,
Strike deep their roots before their flowers unfold.

The vines of nature ask the culturing hand,
To lift their tendrils in the noon-tide blaze,—
Nor less the germs of intellect demand,
Both reason's culture, and truth's genial rays.

---

* These stanzas were written in early life, at a time when the author felt it his duty to renounce, for a time, the cultivation of poetry.

Oh! then, if fancy hath presum'd too soon
To pluck the fruits, or flowers in opening bloom,
I'll wait the hour when manhood's fervid noon,
To those gives richness, and to these perfume.

Then fare-thee-well, my Harp!—and should I not
Again on earth attune thy lays to love;
When these shall perish,—like myself—forgot,
Oh! mayst thou wake to nobler strains above.

DEVOTIONAL POEMS.

I.

TEACH me, oh! Father, good and wise,
The paths of folly to despise,
   And shun the snares of youth;
May all my thoughts incline to thee,
For thou canst set the sinner free,
   And clothe him with thy truth.

And when I feel thy chastening rod,
I'll praise thee still, for thou art God,
   And knowest what is right;
Though darkness may obscure my way,
I'll watch to see the dawning ray,
   Of thy Eternal Light.

For when the soul submits to thee,
This light within she then may see,
   And own thy way is best;
The Christian then enraptur'd cries,
While grateful tears start from his eyes,
   How are the righteous blest!

Though Death stride victor through the land,
Upheld by thy Almighty Hand,
   Still do they trust in thee,—
For well they know that all thy ways,
Shall call forth everlasting praise,
   When Time shall cease to be.

II.

GRANT me, once more, Almighty Lord,
   To supplicate thy throne of grace,—
Withdraw not yet thy precious word,—
   From me, oh! hide not now thy face.

My foes encompass me around,
   On every side their arrows fly;
Heal,—heal, O Lord, the mortal wound,
   Emmanuel save me, or I die.

'Tis all in vain I arm my heart
   With firm resolves to shun the snare,
The tempter comes with subtle art,
   Corrupts the guard, and enters there.

Thy temple, Lord, have they defil'd,
   Thine altars have they broken down,—
The place where once thy beauty smil'd,
   Now seems o'erclouded with thy frown.

Once more wilt thou, my Saviour, deign
   To bless me with thy smile benign,
Oh! wilt thou yet consent to reign
   Within a heart so frail as mine.

I feel the burden of my sin,
   Abhor the masters I have served,—
Thine eye hath all my anguish seen,
   And all my bitter tears observed.

Oh! fix within my heart thy throne,
   From sin's hard bondage set me free,
I'll place my trust on thee alone,
   And all my soul devote to thee.

III.

Oh! thou Almighty Power above,
   And sovereign Lord of all,
Continue still thy work of love,
   Preserve me, or I fall.

'Twas thou alone didst set me free
   From Egypt's darksome land;
The powers of sin, in judgment's sea,
   Were whelm'd at thy command.

My tongue was loos'd to sing thy praise,
    In that delightful hour,—
Thy goodness, and thy boundless grace,
    Thy majesty and power.

Oh! Lamb of God, continue still,
    To bless me with thy love,
Deign thou my hungering soul to fill
    With manna from above.

And oh! be pleased, my raging thirst,
    With water to assuage,
Which flows from thee, my only trust,
    The Rock of every age.

———

IV.

Oh! when, ye Passions, will ye cease
    To rend my aching heart with pain,—
Oh! when wilt thou, celestial Peace,
    Return and rest with me again?
    Long have I striven, but in vain,
To quell each rising, vain desire,—
    Oh! come, Emmanuel, come and reign,—
A purer, brighter flame inspire,
And cause my heart to glow, with thy own heavenly
        fire.

Does there remain a place for me,
    Within the bounds of Zion's hill?
Can such a sinner yet be free,—
    Oh! may he hope for pardon still?
    Lord, let me bow before thy will,
Oh! condescend to hear my prayer;
    Teach me each duty to fulfil,
And guard me from each secret snare;
My heart with love refine, and fix thy kingdom there.

———

V.

GREAT Source of life and purity,
    All human praise excelling,
Whose empire is infinity,
    The humble heart thy dwelling.

The winds and waves confess thy might,
    Which curbs the raging ocean,
Which bade the planets spring to light,
    And still directs their motion.

All nature owns thy sovereign sway,
    From thee each power deriving,
Shall man alone then disobey,
    With whom thy spirit's striving.

On him alone hast thou conferr'd
   Each high and holy feeling,
The riches of thy living word,
   Within his heart revealing.

Oh! let me then devote to thee,
   The powers which thou hast given,—
And may they all incentives be,
   To lead my soul to heaven.

THE ACTIVITY OF THE SOUL.

My slumb'ring soul, awake, arise,
The dream of life will soon be ended,—
Remember, there are brighter skies,
      For man intended.

The journey to that glorious sphere,
Must be through toil and self-denying,
For while we stand or loiter here,
      Our time is flying.

Look round the world, and say, if aught
Has been created void of motion,—
See! how the winds, with blessings fraught,
      Sweep o'er the ocean.

Without their pure and potent breath,
The slumb'ring waves, in foul stagnation,
Would send forth pestilential death,
      O'er all creation.

'Tis thus, to rouse the soul to bliss,
A power invisible is given,
Within the world of mind,—it is
        The breath of Heaven.

See! what a stream of light comes forth
From yon bright sun, continual flowing,—
Cheer'd by his smile, th' obedient earth
        Is onward going.

But oh! there is a sun more bright,
To works of love the soul inclining,—
Tho' oft by clouds obscured, His light
        Is ever shining.

His word shall evermore endure,—
His presence, every good comprises,
And every aspiration pure,
        From Him arises.

For human souls the course how clear!
While they pursue the path of duty,
Like planets, moving in their sphere
        Of heavenly beauty.

Oh! then let not the soul stand still,
While all creation is in motion,
But, by obedience to His will,
        Prove our devotion.

And while on its probation here,
Th' attentive mind His law is learning,—
Still, to a higher, nobler sphere,
     Its thoughts are turning.

And ev'n in purer realms above,
Can there be bliss, without employment?
Oh no! the soul, in deeds of love,
     Will find enjoyment.

Throughout creation, all we see,
Is this important lesson teaching,—
The soul must ever active be,
     And forward reaching.

How vast a field of wonders here,
By Heavenly love has been provided,
To prompt the mind, in its career
     By Science guided.

But far more glorious the abode,
Prepar'd on high for our reception,
And nobler powers will be bestow'd
     For its perception.

And oh! methinks, in that blest clime,
The soul redeemed, with rapture burning,—
In wisdom, more and more sublime,
     Will still be learning.

Then, forward let us take our way,
No longer " slumber's chain" should bind us,
But all that would our march delay,
      Be cast behind us.

Not for the gain of sordid gold,
Nor worldly power, be our endeavour;
For if to these in bondage sold,
      We're lost forever.

Not to the field of martial strife,
For man's applause, our course directing,—
But for a higher, purer life,
      Our powers perfecting.

The church of Christ—his spotless bride,
Invites us, in the martyr's story,—
His spirit too—our light and guide,
      Calls us to glory.

Whose faith shall to the end endure,
O'er all the powers of sin victorious,
A crown of life shall there secure,
      Forever glorious.

And he, who while sojourning here,
One wandering soul from sin shall sever,
There, like a planet in his sphere,
      Shall shine forever.

1839.

THE END.

CPSIA information can be obtained at www.ICGtesting.com
Printed in the USA
BVOW071602051111

275346BV00001B/214/A

9 780548 625217